EXCAVATIONS
AND THEIR OBJECTS

EXCAVATIONS
AND THEIR OBJECTS

Freud's
Collection of Antiquity

EDITED BY

Stephen Barker

STATE UNIVERSITY OF NEW YORK PRESS

Published by
State University of New York Press, Albany

© 1996 State University of New York

For information, address State University of New York
Press, State University Plaza, Albany, N.Y., 12246

Production by Diane Ganeles
Marketing by Fran Keneston

Library of Congress Cataloging-in-Publication Data

Excavations and their objects : Freud's collection of Antiquity /
    edited by Stephen Barker.
        p.   cm.
    Includes bibliographical references and index.
    ISBN 0-7914-2293-3 (acid-free). — ISBN 0-7914-2294-1 (pbk. : acid
-free)
    1. Freud, Sigmund, 1856–1939—Exhibitions.   2. Freud, Sigmund,
1856–1939—Archaeological collections—Exhibitions.   3. Freud
Museum—Exhibitions.   4. Antiquities—Private collections—England—
London—Exhibitions.   5. Psychoanalysis and art—Exhibitions.
I. Barker, Stephen, 1946– .
AM401.F74E93   1996
069'.5'07442142—dc20   94-8842
                                                                    CIP

10   9   8   7   6   5   4   3   2   1

Contents

Introduction

After the death of his father in 1896, Sigmund Freud embarked on one of the most fascinating and dramatic journeys of his life. The journey was not to other countries than Austria, nor to other cities than Vienna (though those journeys, later in Freud's life, proved to be very dramatic in themselves)—indeed, Freud's journey took place not in space but in time: after Jacob's death, Sigmund Freud began a strategic and concerted journey "back" through the rich and diverse cultural history Freud had inherited and which he fashioned for himself. This journey manifested itself, interestingly, in Freud's beginning in 1896 to collect an ever-growing accumulation of art objects from around the world, chiefly from Greece, Rome, and China. Each of the pieces Freud bought had a special association for him, telling part of the story of the culture Freud saw as symbolically contained in and articulated by them, and of which he was both a part and a spokesperson.

As the young Freud's collection, most significantly consisting of small statuary but containing many other kinds of art objects as well, grew in size (eventually to over two thousand pieces), it also continued to grow in importance to Freud. In 1938, as he was forced to contemplate leaving Vienna in order to avoid what by that time had become inevitable Nazi persecution, he became increasingly preoccupied with the problematics of keeping his treasured collection around him, and deeply worried as to whether the Nazis would allow its—or, after all, his own—departure from Austria. Freud's concern over the maintaining of his collection superseded many seemingly more pressing and vital ones. For weeks, he anxiously awaited authorization to emigrate with his beloved collection. Then, on 23 May, 1938, he received word that the objects had been released, and (because they had been intentionally underestimated in value by a sympathetic appraiser) amazingly for only a small fee. Greatly relieved, Freud moved to London, into his new and final home in Maresfield Gardens, and reestablished, for what turned out to be the last year of his life, his accustomed place within the maze of statues and other objects he had so assiduously collected. For that last short period, his life could continue almost as it had been before his forced move, a source of great comfort to Freud, as he repeatedly declared and wrote.

On the death of Freud's daughter Anna in 1982, the residence in Hampstead had been bequeathed to the English Charity for preservation, and had finally become the Freud Museum in 1986. Freud's study in the Hampstead house was then, and is now, just as it was at his death in September 1939, all of the over two thousand pieces he collected over those forty-odd years in the places Freud had designated for them. What had always had something of the air of tomb, with its various reliquaries, had now become a museum instead. In 1987, Lynn Gamwell, Director of the University Art Museum at SUNY-Binghamton, discovered that no significant part of the collection had left Freud's study since its installation there in 1938. Realizing that the collection was a far too well-kept secret, and that it represented a fascinating window on an aspect of Freud not otherwise available, Dr. Gamwell, in conjunction with Richard Wells, Director of the Freud Museum, organized a travelling exhibition of sixty-seven of the collection's antiquities, sponsored by CIBA-GEIGY and the National Endowment for the Arts. In addition, Dr. Gamwell and Mr. Wells produced a remarkable catalogue for the travelling exhibit, combining plates and histories of the chosen pieces with essays about the collection by Freud scholars and art historians and critics.

Dr. Gamwell also arranged or suggested the arrangement, in many of the sites of its display during its American tour, of symposia related to Freud's art objects, to Freud's collecting, or to his work in general. Numerous of these symposia took place, across the country in 1990 and 1991, during the tour. The great majority of them were in the end medical in nature; they addressed issues having to do with Freud's place in the medical or the psychoanalytic community, paying less attention to the objects that had catalyzed the symposia in the first place, and to the urge in Freud that had made collecting (and gathering *this* collection) so central to his adult life.

When I began to organize the symposium which would accompany and highlight the visit of the travelling exhibition of Freud's collection to the Art Gallery of the University of California, Irvine campus in November 1990, I knew that I wanted to do several rather different things with it. First, I wanted to gather a small group of diverse academics and scholars to discuss the theoretical and historical dimensions of Freud's aesthetic itself, as evidenced by the actual objects on display in the Gallery, in an informal but concentrated setting that would offer potential visitors to the exhibition the opportunity to study the pieces on display and to hear commentary about them and their place in Freud's aesthetic, as well as professional, life. And I wanted to ensure that the symposium presentations would reach a wider audience, since it is my strong view that an understanding of Freud's collecting, indeed of his larger aesthetic sense, is vitally important to a greater understanding of his work and thought as an innovator and psychoanalyst. SUNY Press and the diligence of Carola Sautter, the acquisitions editor of this volume, have now seen to that objective.

I want to offer special thanks to Peter A. Gelker, M. D., for his assistance in alerting the psychoanalytic community about the symposium.

This volume contains reworked versions of all the presentations at that small symposium. Each of the contributors has a remarkably different tack to take with regard to the importance, impetus, and interpretation of Freud's aesthetic from all the others; this in itself I look on as a most felicitous part of any meaningful response to the theme of archaeology and the collecting of antiquities as practiced by Freud. The symposium turned out to be provocative and engaging, well worth doing on numerous levels. The findings of the presentations are valid beyond the presence of the antiquities

that inspired them. The figures with which Freud surrounded himself in Vienna and then in London have a great deal to say about his
sensibility, his subtlety, his links to the past, and his theoretical
models.

On this larger scale the archaeological theme announced in
the volume's title and its playful reference to objects of archaeology
(both in terms of abstract goals and concrete discoveries) is so pervasive in Freud, and indeed in all scientific thought at least since Ar-
istotle, that its use here is justified chiefly by the metaphor's
remarkable aptness to the strategies of psychology and psychoanalysis as developed by Freud. The power of the archaeological metaphor, explored by Donald Kuspit at length in the travelling
exhibition's catalogue,[1] has several purposes in Freudian thought.
First and foremost is to ground psychology and psychoanalysis
in science, and thereby to "ingratiate psychoanalysis with society" (133). This ingratiation consists for Freud of a ratification of
the seriousness and solidity of psychoanalysis as a discipline and a
purposive engendering of sympathy and support for a nascent discipline of inquiry into self-understanding. For Freud, this self-
understanding, on the individual and internal level, is no different
from the external and collective activity of the archaeologist. Indeed, Freud thought of psychoanalysis as in no way different from
archaeology; they were for him versions of the same thing: both ob-
ject-related human sciences. Human reality, for Freud—both the
mundane, day-to-day reality of lived human experience and the abstracted, metaphorical reality required for any concept of "self," is
founded on the past and on the stories and legends by which we individually and collectively come to know ourselves. To investigate
the individual reality of the ego (which is itself a story: the story of
the "I am") is to attempt to uncover the influences and impetuses
of the past, and then to read them into the present and project them
into the future. Since fully-lived, adult reality is for Freud a question of maintaining this layered, narrative sense of reality, and fos-
tering the tendentious continuity of past, present, and future, it
must be structured in and evaluatable by science, that is by a con-

certed and homogeneous methodology. Thus the roots of psychoanalysis and archaeology are identical; Freud's deep admiration for
Schliemann, the discoverer of Troy, can come as no surprise.[2]

And yet Freud's seemingly simplistic view of the relation between psychoanalysis and archaeology is actually much more complex than its surface would suggest. Like the Freudian psyche, the
metaphor of archaeology is for Freud infinitely layered, and therefore consists of much more than meets the eye. In fact, one of the
most vital aspects of the archaeological metaphor for psychoanalysis, as it is employed by Freud, is its dialectic of concealment and
revelation. Freud's view that objects from the past, like memories,
both reveal and conceal that past informs his psychoanalytic inquiry, structuring it around the constant analysis of a yet uncovered
and even unremembered past, revealed only indirectly and very partially in its manifestations, be they general and specific behaviors,
narratives of dreams, or the collecting of objects of antiquity. Central to Freud's genius is the realization that to discover, reveal, or
create an interpretation or narrative of any part of the remembered
past is to metamorphose it; to transpose an object from the past
into a narrated present is to bring it into a renewed present, a new
reality. In this respect, Freud reveals himself to be every inch the
scientist, clearly following a schematic notion of "scientia," knowledge, back so to speak through the archaeological metaphor to its
"original object," the memory-trace from which it springs but which
it may no longer resemble nor contain except as part of a narrative
fiction, albeit a narrative with a very powerful *present* validity.

The carefully-chosen objects with which Freud surrounded
himself in his Hampstead study evoked and tantalized, offering a
remnant or trace of other times and places while acting as markers
for those times and places, as indices of absence but with the recon-
stitutive power of their centrality to his present narrative of the
valid and meaningful past. Indeed, Freud was so greatly drawn to
and charmed by the objects he had gathered around him that, sitting at his desk with that array of tiny friends before him, he posited
in them the collective psyche of aesthetic culture. This is particularly interesting since the objects' "value," aside from their market

value as antiquities, emanated from their suggestion and establish-
ment of meaning, written "through" their objectness to a nearly,
and in some cases wholly, forgotten past and time.

And so again, in this respect as in so many others, psychoanalysis and archaeology are indeed identical, and are indeed undone by
only one unscientific thing: meaninglessness. Freud himself, of
course, made numerous direct references to the similarities between these two sciences, in part to validate psychoanalysis and in
part because the metaphor connecting the two—that of excavation
of something meaningful which is concealed behind or beneath an
obscurant surface—is so apt; what is generally *not* recognized
about Freud's well-known penchant for the archaeological metaphor is that *as a metaphor* it indicates precisely the sort of narrative
power Freud reserves for it, far beyond the physical objects on which
archaeology concentrates. For Freud, the objects archaeology un-
earths are not central objects, but rather those iconic objects as catalysts for narratives within which they will be framed. The lesson of
archaeology and psychoanalysis is that in learning to read, and even
more actively to narrate, these markers of the past, we validate
(while imagining or inventing) our own past, as a hypothetically
logical conduit to the lived present and the projected future, and begin to form a vital relationship between the seemingly glimpsed
past and its motivating remnants in (or stories of) present life.

That Freud the metaphorical archaeologist collected aesthetically pleasing objects further compounds their tendentious power.
Freud's view of the psyche contains such a dark side, such a Nietzschean perspective on the forces of which we are constituted, that
even for us to view the objects with which he so dramatically surrounded himself is to become aware of a telling omission among
the objects Freud actually collected and the objects, as a whole, that
might be available to be collected. Only a very limited segment of
the Freudian psyche is represented in Freud's collection, because
the very nature of such iconic images, in a cultural context such as
the one Freud explores in *Civilization and Its Discontents* and elsewhere, limits to the "beautiful" the perimeters of what such objects
may depict, and what may be remembered (the theme of what is and
is not "contained" or "marked" in the objects Freud collected is ad-

dressed in each of the essays in this volume). Thus archaeology, in this case unlike psychoanalysis, shows its limitations as itself a marker of the human psyche, and depicts, rather, the cultural and societal normatives by which that fuller psyche is suppressed.

This volume carries the Freudian notion of metaphorical interpretation and the narrative excavation of history to the critical level. Though they manifest many common themes, the volume's six essays represent a wide variety of responses to Freud, his collection, and the context in which one might view it and him in terms of both aesthetics and cultural archaeology. A thread of continuity is formed by the fact that, as was the case in the symposium at UC—Irvine in which the papers originated, the central idea in each presentation is that of responding to the aesthetics and the theory of Freud's collection, as well as to the thematics of collecting itself as an aesthetic and an autoaesthetic activity.[3] As a result of this desire for a close connection with the objects Freud collected, and with the theoretical context in which he *concealed* the reasons for their assemblage, in all of the following essays reference is made and much specific attention is paid to individual pieces in the collection itself; where appropriate here, illustrations punctuate the narrative to allow greater insight into these specifics. The volume moves generally from considerations of Freud's biographical context "out" to those of a more theoretical nature, though each of the essays contains elements of both.

In the volume's first essay, "A Collector Analyzes Collecting: Sigmund Freud on the Passion to Possess," Lynn Gamwell, the original curator and compiler of the exhibit, introduces the main themes of the volume and sets the stage for further investigation by detailing the collection's inception and history, and by excavating and examining Freud's passion for collecting which, as Dr. Gamwell points out, was as powerful in Freud as his much-discussed addiction to smoking. Establishing them as a core of the evidence for Freud's need to collect, Dr. Gamwell directs our attention to the figures immediately in front of Freud at his writing desk, analyzes their significance, and provides fascinating details of their meaning to Freud and to culture in general. Calling the figures on Freud's desk his "audience," as he himself did, Dr. Gamwell evokes the strong forces Freud drew from these iconic figures as he himself explored unknown, or at least unarticulated, substrata of the psyche. The eerie powers of past and present invoked in the designation of this cluster of small statues as "listeners" to Freud's discourse with his own *internal* cultural history, as it is evoked in his written work, are considerable. Dr. Gamwell's broad familiarity with the collection, piece by piece and as a whole, lends a powerful grounding to the interpretive essays to follow. Dr. Gamwell does considerable interpretation herself, of course, laying out a case for Freud's passion to "possess" his artifacts and its origins in his personality and desire for recognition and legitimation.

Dr. Peter Loewenberg, a practicing psychoanalyst as well as a professor of history at UCLA, explores in "The Pagan Freud" the "cultural identity" Freud formed—and transformed—out of his Jewish heritage, both in terms of its assimilation (and sublimation) into his life and work, and of his overt rejection of that heritage as a way of life. Investigating what he calls Freud's "indifference" to any theistic system, as extensively expressed by Freud, Dr. Loewenberg makes a case for Freud's art collecting as a deeply meaningful and symbolic alternative to religion and spirituality, both because the collected pieces are "cultic and totemic figures" in their own right and because Freud himself infused them with an intense spiritual significance vis-à-vis his own work and thought. In Dr. Loewenberg's analysis of Freud's collection and collecting, Freud's very complicated attitude toward the objects of antiquity, as well as the kind of reality he ascribed to them, informs his inversion of religion and paganism such that the pagan (e.g., pagan Rome) is revered while the Christian (here Christian Rome) is vilified as a sham. Weaving together a series of Freud's statements on antiquity and paganism, ranging from early in his life to the very threshold of his death, Dr. Loewenberg creates a rich and dense texture of evidence to support his case that Freud was himself a stoic and stubborn pagan to the very end, unswervingly devoted to principles meaningful to him but without illusions concerning the spirituality, indeed the very reality, of human life. Dr. Loewenberg's is a portrait of a long-suffering and benevolent Freud for whom aesthetics and art collecting satisfied a deep need for practical fortitude and creative stimulus.

Juliet Flower MacCannell, in her "Signs of the Fathers: Freud's Collection of Antiquities," excavates a series of symbolic and semiotic themes within Freud's larger collection of figures, and then within the smaller collection chosen for touring, taking as a framework an exploration of various aspects of Freud's passion for collecting itself, within the context established by Neo-Freudian analysis, in particular that of Jacques Lacan and his concept of the *object a* and the fetish. Dr. MacCannell shows that collecting itself is fetishization and that, indeed, "Neo-Freudianism" as a discipline is itself a function of the archaeological metaphor, since its developments capitalize on the hidden (i.e., semiotic) aspects of Freud's own declared theories and open Freud's work to new ages and angles of critical reaction. Thus, a dialogue between Freud and the Neo-Freudians—chiefly Lacan—might produce in its own right a very provocative (re-)analysis of central Freudian themes. Dr. MacCannell's double interest, in Freud as a collector and Lacan as the theorist of the father-fetish, leads to consideration of the centrality and power of figurality in general and in specific to the nature of the iconic figure, and finally to the place and value of heavily invested figures of antiquity, for Freud.

According to Dr. MacCannell's interpretation, a kind of biological and super-biological evolution can be seen in Freud's figures. Noting the large number of animal figures in Freud's collection, Dr. MacCannell analyzes the developmental stages of Freud's figure collecting, from those of pre-humans (e.g., monkey figures) at one end of the spectrum, to those representing the superhuman (the "narcissistic superego") at the other, showing how animal figures operated for Freud as indices and markers of "the limits on and of the human" in Freudian theory, always in concert with figures linked to the superego, as the opposite limit of the human. As fetish figures defining the human relative to the animal or pre-human, Freud's collection is symbolically important to his theories, in terms of his strategies of hidden and revealed signs, both as totemic figures for the sub-rational forces with which we must deal as animals ourselves, and the cultural or super-individual forces by which we regulate behavior and establish an ego-sense as rational beings. Dr. MacCannell selects a series of pieces from the travelling collection and analyzes them in order to demonstrate how Freud's figures established for him a set of "ideals" within which ties between individual and community could be forged; then, within the context of this same set of selected pieces, Dr. MacCannell extends her investigation to the broader question inherent in Freud's collection and its significance: the question as to the nature of the very sexual identity men and women experience in this Freudian and Neo-Freudian context. Reminding us that in terms of the concept of sexual identity, that is to say in more strictly evolutionary terms, Freud's "real 'Father' was a monkey—that [humankind's] divinely ideal genealogy is no more than a "descent from the lower animals"—Freud attempts to correct in us any illusions of a perfected or perfectible human state as attainable or indeed desirable. Given this grounding of the human in the "pre-human," Dr. MacCannell shows how Freud's correction of human aspiration to perfection extends for Freud even to such a powerful model of a perfectible humanity as that conceived in Hegel's idealization of rationality.

Thus art, and the act of collecting art, in the context Dr. MacCannell defines for them, are finally at the same time both great contextualizers and generators of dialectic; art and collecting act as powerful reminders of the perpetual medial position we must always occupy within the spectrum of conceivable human possibilities, caught (to paraphrase Nietzsche) between beast and superego. In this context, art and the activity of its collecting travel well beyond the usual aesthetic sphere; both are indeed useful and telling as semiotic markers, just as both art and collecting are meaningfully evocative as catalysts for deeper and richer self-definition.

Capitalizing on a set of themes introduced in the volume by Dr. MacCannell, Kenneth Reinhard in "The Freudian Things: Construction and the Archaeological Metaphor" focuses on the relationship among Freud, Lacan, the unconscious, and the psychoanalytic object, as extrapolated from the archaeological objects with which Freud surrounded himself. In the Lacanian development and refiguring of Freud, particularly in terms of the unconscious and its relation to the object as such, as Reinhard points out, the archaeological metaphor so often associated not only with Freud's art collecting but with his psychoanalytic theory in general undergoes a very significant transformation: no longer is the psychoanalyst's delving into the unconscious to be seen as the anticipated uncovering of objects by which we as observers, like the patient, can accrue greater and greater personal insight into person and process, but rather as indeed a perpetual loss and re-loss of the unconscious itself, as a "primary rupture." In the psychoanalytic search itself, Reinhard maintains, are the precise conditions of its displacement. This "Orphic" (or, indeed, Romantic) archaeology, according to Lacan, in which we search and never find, re-defines the "Freudian Thing" in terms of what is lost (and, in our growing understanding of the real conditions of the search, what is therefore found) in Freud's art collecting and his technique for psychoanalysis. Dr. Reinhard points out the divergences between the (psycho)analytic and the archaeological in light of this altered perspective, and by extension faces the problems associated with the orchestrating of the strategic archaeological metaphor for Freud, suggesting that rather than being merely a metaphor, the archaeological analogy works in Freud's view more as an allegory for the *desired* discoveries of the analyst. In the attempt to lift the veils of repression concealing meanings unavailable to conscious process, and to our struggles to find them, the analyst destroys them, leaving only remnants (memorials) to both meanings and repression. Resolution of the dichotomy between psychoanalysis and archaeology can occur, according to Lacan and Reinhard, within the context of the strategy of (re)construction employed, finally, by both. Reinhard cites Freud's contemporary, Walter Benjamin, on the notion of construction as the creating of a theoretical "constellation" recognizable only in the narration of its totality, and yet which by its very nature is always non-totalized, a matter of perspective. Finally, citing the fact that Freud's final archaeological marker, his own ashes, reside in one of his own ancient urns, Reinhard draws on Benjamin to show that collecting is a "determination of the collector by the things whose possession itself possesses him." For Reinhard, as for Lacan and Freud, our struggle for a coherent theoretical comprehension of the "thing" results in our determination by it.

My own essay, like Dr. Reinhard's, addresses the notion of the constellation relative to Freud's collection and his worldview, but instead of exploring the theoretical forces contributing to Freud's zeal for collecting I investigate the cluster of abstracted iconic figures standing, as markers, in hypothetical juxtaposition to the figures on Freud's desk and around his study. Given Freud's fascination with the "past in the present," my hypothesis is that one can perceive, in Freud's collected figures, a kinship and relation to some absent figures in his own genealogical past whose magnetic pull attests to their power in formulating Freud's aesthetic. My contention is that Freud's passion for collecting and the objects manifesting it represent a complex web of self-empowering strategies gathered in totemic fashion around a clearly discernable set of psychological and aesthetic criteria; Freud, I maintain, invents and defines himself through his collecting, establishing a basis for the power of thought and writing in the amassed statuary with which he surrounded himself. My essay's strategy is to gather together, in a similar sense to that in which Dr. Reinhard uses it, a constellation—a critical mass of ancient narrative power, suspended in those iconic figures before Freud but suggesting and evoking several others not physically represented in the art Freud collected. I identify a "Pentateuch" of such genealogically empowering figures, from whom I contend Freud had to draw power and then distance himself: Freud's (dead) father Jakob; the Moses of the Philippson Bible, which Freud knew well through biblical text and illustration; the Moses of Michelangelo, about which Freud had so much to say throughout his life; Friedrich Nietzsche, who Freud declares he had to reject in order to have his own thoughts; and the Nietzschean concept of the *Übermensch,* the ideal, self-sufficient figure of authority, so centrally important to Freud, as a scientist and as a person, as well. Through a suggestive investigation of the theme of autoaesthetics, the essay aims to show that Freud had a powerful strategy, highly aesthetic and multi-layered, behind the form and content of his collection of antiquities, in which he showed himself to be deeply immersed, and which relates closely to his psychoanalytic strategies and values as well. In his need to establish himself as an autonomous figure of authority, Freud privileged other such figures which, in their own ways, became for him the iconic display of that self-formulative power. In adopting this strategy of sublimation and transference, Freud inadvertently collaborated with that figure from whom he said he had to divorce himself: Nietzsche. In this collaboration, Freud subtly set a tone, along with Nietzsche, for the aesthetization of the twentieth century.

Julia Lupton, in her essay "Sphinx with Bouquet," is also interested in Freud's collection from the point of view of what its aesthetics and its selectivity reveals about its collector. She investigates Freud's notion of science and of the interweaving of the sciences, and Freud's discriminating taste, chronicling, thematizing, and distinguishing between items chosen and other items not chosen for collection by Freud—and then, at another level, objects chosen and not chosen for inclusion in the very abbreviated travelling version of the collection compiled by Dr. Gamwell and Mr. Wells. Dr. Lupton centers her investigation on Freud's sphinx figures, including the cover-image for the catalogue accompanying the exhibit, as the enigmatic markers by which to distinguish Freud's cross-disciplinary and inter-scientific interest. Detailing Freud's process of selection, Dr. Lupton cites this process as the articulation of an underlying biological sanction for psychoanalysis, a "language of flowers" Freud employs to mark and transcend "a series of linked distinctions" such as botany and aesthetics, narrative and decorative arts, repression and sublimation. Underlying her own investigation is the grounding notion of the "flowering" of Freudian thought, in the formulation of the ideas out of which psychoanalysis grew and blossomed. Inherent in this process, Dr. Lupton claims, is the pivotal Freudian imagery of the symbolism of flowers themselves in the process of development and growth: for Freud, flowers stand for or mean meaning itself.

Dr. Lupton shows that the sphinx and the bouquet typify the two aspects of Freud's aesthetic theory. The essay makes the case for a telling parallel between the two central sphinxes in Freud's collection (the "Oedipal" one shown on the cover of the exhibition catalogue and the "à la grecque" sphinx with bouquet left behind in Freud's study) and the Freudian concepts of repression and sublimation. Calling on the Kantian notion of the flower as emblem of "free beauty," Lupton draws a line from Kant through Linneaus' "sexual system" of flowers to Freud's distinction between repressed and sublimated sexuality, in dreams and beyond in psychic life. Positing collecting, the "uncanny maternal crossroads" between repression and sublimation, as the focus of Freud's science, Dr. Lupton shows how "sphinx with bouquet" becomes the sublimated equivalent of "Freud with Kant." Finally, the essay demonstrates the connection between the sublime sexuality of flower imagery and the sphinx within the Freudian context, on the one hand, and the image of the Medusa as a related condensation of apocryphal "maternal phalli," on the other, never really "there" but always an emblem for the repressed.

The *leitmotif* of all the volume's essays is that while Freud's collection of antiquities reveals a great deal about him, it conceals even more than it reveals about his psyche, his history and tradition, and the processes of the mind. To give this formulation a Heideggerian turn, the collection reveals what is *not* concealed within it, even while it defines what is concealed there. In some respect, the art objects with which Freud surrounded himself act as a better—because more elliptical, suggestive, and imagistic— marker for the mechanism of psychoanalysis than any other source; indeed, as good a one as Freud's writings themselves. Because Freud's iconic statues are objects, *things,* Freud's art engages us at a different level than his erudite (and thus more conscious) work. We can learn a great deal about Freud's psychic makeup, and by extension our own, by looking closely at Freud's collection and the strategies that amassed it. This volume offers a first gesture toward such a closer look.

1

A Collector Analyses Collecting: Sigmund Freud on the Passion to Possess

Lynn Gamwell

The father of psychoanalysis was a passionate collector of ancient art. Sigmund Freud assembled a museum-quality collection of over two thousand ancient Egyptian, Greek, Roman, and Asian objects, over a period of forty years. Informed by his extensive archaeological library, he acquired these artifacts and had them authenticated by experts at the Kunsthistorisches Museum in Vienna. One of his patients remembers that analytic sessions with Freud were not so much like going to a doctor's office as like entering a museum.[1]

Art collectors such as Freud often express a strong emotional attachment to their acquisitions. Collecting is their "addiction" and acquiring some object was an "irresistible impulse." They "fell in love" with the piece and "couldn't live without it." Why do people collect art with such passion?

Although Freud himself collected only rather inexpensive objects on his modest income, the history of museums is thick with collectors who were willing to spend vast fortunes on art. In recent years, collectors have paid $40.7 million for Picasso's *Au Lapin Agile* and $82.5 million for Van Gogh's *Portrait of Dr. Gachet*. What motivates collectors to spend so much money?

These questions are raised in the vast recent literature about private, corporate, and museum collections, which is found throughout publications that cover art or finance. Reasons given for why people collect include prestige, self-expression, fame, spiritual needs, investment, and image-building. What is lacking in this literature is a psychoanalytic explanation of these reasons, in terms of both the passion people feel for collecting, and the consistent association, today and throughout history, of art and money.

In this essay I will first look to Freud—the psychoanalyst and collector—for insight into the psychology of collecting, and then turn to Freud's own collection as an example of "the passion to possess."

The Psychology of Collecting

What did the founder of psychoanalysis and avid art collector tell us about the psychology of collecting? Unfortunately Freud rarely mentioned his personal collecting, and he never stated directly what any of his individual pieces meant to him. Throughout his writing, Freud made an analogy of archaeology and psychoanalysis, both reconstructions of the past from buried fragments, but only very rarely did Freud relate that analogy to his *own* archaeological collection.[2] Some of his antiquities have an obvious link to his theories—a Greek vase depicting Oedipus and the Sphinx, a terracotta statue of Eros—but most do not. Also, in his theoretical writing, Freud only rarely referred to collecting as a psychological phenomenon. Freud's curious silence on this topic is in keeping with his sense of privacy and unwillingness to expose his personal life in other areas, such as in the interpretation of his own dreams.[3]

However, if we examine the few remarks which Freud did make, we find him clearly pointing to the psychological roots of all collecting as being grounded in sensual pleasure. Simply put, collecting *is* a passion. Freud related the adult passion for collecting to pleasures deriving ultimately from the three zones of the body which, according to Freud, are the focus of sexual attention at different stages of development: the oral, the anal and the genital. Freud's libidinal explanation of psychosexual development has been found incomplete by later psychoanalysts, and Freud's theory has been revised specifically as it relates to collecting objects by authors such as D. W. Winnicott.[4] However, in this essay I would like to focus on Freud's own theoretical writing and collecting and give an exposition of his original and highly influential views as they relate to the psychology of collecting. Typical of Freud's approach, we find him tracing adult activities with "high" intellectual content to their most primitive sources, rooted in the pleasures of breast-feeding, retaining feces, and stimulation of the genitals.

Does this mean that the great art collections of the world can be reduced to manifestations of suckling, constipation and lust? Hardly. Adult activities, whatever their origins, also incorporate the intellectual pursuits and contemporary experiences of mature men and women. Freud's own collection is infused with intellectual meaning related to his adult professional life, as I will discuss below.[5] However to understand Freud's views on the emotional roots of collecting, we must return with him to its unsuppressed childhood origins in a search for pleasure: oral, anal and genital erotism.

An Addiction

Freud understood smoking, along with other oral pleasures such as thumb-sucking and kissing, as a way to satisfy the desire to repeat the infant's first sensual satisfaction, oral pleasure in suckling. The early origin of this desire partially explains why it is so profound and why its satisfaction is so addictive. Freud called his art collecting an addiction comparable to his smoking habit, although less intense.[6] He experienced collecting and smoking as similarly irresistible impulses.

A Desire to Retain

In Freud's classic essay "Character and Anal Erotism" of 1908, which is the only piece of Freud's writing ever cited in subsequent discussions of the psychological origins of collecting,[7] Freud describes three character traits commonly found together in adults— orderliness, parsimony, and obstinacy—as sublimations of the second type of sensual pleasure, anal erotism, which is pleasure associated with defecating. Specifically, parsimony is an adult sublimation of childhood anal pleasure in holding in feces.

Stinginess has two aspects, the refusal to give and the desire
to retain. The latter is found in the collector, who gathers various
adult symbols of feces, most commonly money.

Freud noticed that "wherever archaic modes of thought have
predominated or persist—in ancient civilizations, in myths, fairy
tales and superstitions, in unconscious thinking, in dreams and in
neuroses—money is brought into the most intimate relationship with filth."[8] We speak of being "filthy rich," "wallowing in
wealth," and tell stories of the goose that laid the golden egg, and
the devil who gave gold to his lovers, which turned to dung on his
departure. Freud speculated that it is perhaps the very contrast of
gold and feces, the most precious and most worthless substances
known to man, that led to their identification,[9] since, according to
his theory, in the unconscious opposites can be equated and represent each other.

Can art also be drawn into this identification? It certainly has
an association with gold; we speak of art as "priceless" and an art
museum as a repository of our "national treasures." Donald Kuspit
has put it more bluntly, "Art is another form of money . . . the museum is the bank."[10] The recently escalating prices paid for art have
led to it being discussed more as "commodity" and "blue chip investment," a phenomenon noted by artists such as Joseph Beuys in
his *Kunst = KAPITAL* [Art = CAPITAL] of 1979 and Hans Haacke
in his piece on the corporate art collection of advertising agency
magnates Saatchi and Saatchi, *Global Marketing* of 1987.

Myths of creation commonly tell of the transmutation of
worthless, formless matter (like feces) into something of special
value: the universe is created from chaos; man is created from clay;
artists, like alchemists, create a precious object from base materials.
Art, like gold, also contrasts with feces; art is the highest creation
of man's mind and spirit as opposed to the lowliest production from
the bowels of his body.

Collectors of archaeological objects, like Freud, have a special
interest in buried treasure. Excavation literally means digging in
dirt/filth and has an incestuous association with exploring the hidden entrances and underground passages of Mother Earth.[11]

A Love of Things

Freud made his first acquisition in 1896, and we know from a 1914 etching of Freud that by this date his desk was crowded with Egyptian and Classical statuettes. (*Illus. 1*) Freud published "Character and Anal Erotism" in 1908, at a time when his own collection was growing rapidly. In this same year he related collecting to the third stage of sexual development, the genital, in the following remark:

Illustration 1.   Sigmund Freud at his desk. Etching and drypoint by Max Pollack, 1914. 18$^7/_8$" x 18$^7/_8$". Photo: Freud Museum, London.

> The core of paranoia is the detachment of the libido from objects.
> A reverse course is taken by the collector who directs his surplus
> libido onto an inanimate object: a love of things.[12]

Caused by an inability to attach the libido to an object other than
oneself (that is, to love and trust someone), paranoia may manifest
itself in extreme suspiciousness. However in normal development,
a human matures from the self-love of childhood to the libidinous
attachment, after puberty, to one of the opposite sex. Similarly, the
collector invests some portion of his or her libido in inanimate objects. Freud refers to the collector's libido as "surplus," meaning
that it is over and above the libido directed at the opposite sex.

Although Freud himself never integrated his various comments on collecting, it is clear from this brief examination that his
remarks point to the roots of art collecting in all three stages in his
scheme of sexual development: oral, anal and genital pleasures. To
consider the phenomenon of collecting as related to all three
stages—rather than just anal, as has been done in the past[13]—illus-
trates Freud's own concept of multiple determination, and rings
true to one's personal experience of both the intensity and complexity of the passion to possess.

Freud's Own Passion to Possess

We know from countless anecdotes that Freud loved his own
antiquities collection passionately. A Viennese art dealer who sold
to Freud for over ten years tells of Freud's delight when he first saw
an Egyptian mummy mask which he bought.[14] Freud's household
maid recalls that he was in the habit of affectionately stroking his
Egyptian marble statue of the Baboon of Thoth, as he did his pet
chows, and, on entering his study each morning, Freud warmly
greeted a statue of a Chinese scholar which sat on his desk.[15] Freud
himself wrote to a friend of buying a Greek vase to cheer himself up
after enduring a painful operation.[16]

As we have seen above, Freud understood the origin of collecting in childhood sensual pleasures, which explains the intensity of
the passion. But to understand the collecting of a particular adult,

we must ask in what mature activities is this primitive passion expressed? In other words, what was driving Freud's particular passion to possess these specific objects? This question, of course, does not have a simple answer. Elsewhere I have discussed the inexhaustible layering of meanings of these objects associated with the origins of Freud's collecting in the 1890s, related to his family, his colleagues and his work. Here I would like to expand on my previous discussion,[17] and focus on one small part of Freud's collection (those on his desk) and one feature of his professional life (his extreme isolation in the early years of his career), and suggest that the two may be linked. From the over 2000 antiquities which Freud owned, he selected around forty Egyptian, Classical, and Chinese figurines for his desk, a third of which seem to point to his profound need for colleagues. These figurines not only embody certain psychoanalytic concepts as one would expect, but—as Freud's daily companions and his most immediate, silent audience—they are a strikingly auspicious and defiant group of surrogate colleagues.

Before looking at these objects, let us review Freud's working environment during the decades in which he collected many of these figures for his desk. In Freud's own description of the early part of his career, there is a sense of isolation which also haunted his later, more successful years. Looking back on the 1890s and the first decade of the twentieth century, during which he wrote *The Interpretation of Dreams* (1900), *The Psychopathology of Everyday Life* (1901), *Three Essays on the Theory of Sexuality* (1905), *Jokes and Their Relation to the Unconscious* (1905), and the case histories of Dora (1905), the Rat Man (1909), and Little Hans (1909), Freud wrote the following accounts of his professional environment:

> For more than ten years after my seperation from [collaborator Josef] Breuer [in the late 1890s] I had no followers. I was completely isolated. In Vienna I was shunned; abroad no notice was taken of me. My *Interpretation of Dreams,* published in 1900, was scarcely reviewed in the technical journals.[18]

> The announcement of my unpleasant discoveries had as its result the severance of the greater part of my human contacts. I felt as though I were despised and universally shunned.[19]

And Freud's biographer has commented on the pervasive anti-Semitism in Vienna during these years.[20]

This ostracism by the medical community, together with defections from within the psychoanalytic ranks by Alfred Adler and Carl Jung, led six analysts and friends of Freud to form a support group for psychoanalysis in 1912, called "The Committee" which they protectively kept a secret. Freud responded to this gesture of support in a 1912 letter to the founder of The Committee, Ernest Jones, "I know there is a boyish and perhaps romantic element in this conception [of a secret society] but perhaps it could be adapted to meet the needs of reality."[21]

Turning now to look at Freud's desk, it is apparent that in this atmosphere of professional rejection and isolation, Freud arranged his desk so that he wrote his revolutionary theories in the presence of an audience of figurines, all facing him, including fearless warriors, wise scholars and gods who ruled the sacred territories of the underworld and dreams.

Freud placed a small bronze *Athena* at the center of his desk. (*Illus. 2* shows Freud's view of his desk, as it looked later in his life. Athena is located between the two carved screens, directly above the lying ram, her raised arm silhouetted in front of the figure in the higher screen.) As goddess of wisdom and war, she reigned with the opposed traits of sound intellect and defiant action which characterize the embattled founder of psychoanalysis himself. This tiny warrior, which has many other complex associations to Freud's views,[22] was Freud's undisputed favorite of his entire collection of over 2000 objects.[23] Freud's desk was also "guarded" by a tall, stiding *Warrior,* wearing a helmet with a long crest, which figures prominently in the 1914 depiction of Freud at his desk (*Illus. 2,* silhouetted against Freud's hand). These choices are in keeping with Freud's defensive professional position and his life-long personal identification with warriors such as Hannibal, the Semitic hero and Moses, the law-giver.[24]

Behind *Athena* at the center of Freud's desk stands a Chinese *Table Screen (Illus. 2)*, which is carved with an open decoration of vines. Such screens are commonly found on the desk of a scholar and are intended to encourage contemplation and escape into an

Illustration 2. Freud's desk showing statuette of Athena, in front of Chinese Scholar's screen. Freud Museum, London.

imaginary world. The very notion of a screen that leads to associations, to escape from that real world into a deeper contemplative
state, recalls Freud's concept of a "screen memory" as "one which
owes its value as a memory not to its own content, but to the relation
existing between the content and some other, that has been suppressed" (*SE,* vol. 3, p. 320). When analyzed, a screen memory leads
to a deeper understanding of the self—the inner psychic landscape.
Freud owned several of these Chinese table screens which traditionally depict only landscapes. It is revealing that for his desk, however,
Freud chose an unusual screen which is inset with the figure of a
scholar. There is a second statue of a Chinese scholar on the right of
Freud's desk which, as I mentioned above, was the one he reportedly
greeted each morning . . . as one would a colleague.

The scholarly companions on Freud's desk also included the
Egyptian bronze statuette of *Ptah,* who is represented as having
created the world by speech and thought alone. (*Illus. 2,* back row,
third from right) The Etruscan *Balsamarium* is a double-headed
figure who has the intellectual advantage of, metaphorically, seeing
in more than one direction. The *Baboon of Thoth* combines an animal god with Thoth, the patron of all things intellectual, particularly writing. (*Illus. 1,* the *Baboon* is in profile, with the half-moon
symbolizing Thoth appearing like a lump on its head, just below
Freud's writing arm)

Dominion over the underworld was represented on Freud's
desk by the bronze head of *Osiris,* also seen in the 1914 etching. (*Illus. 1,* the head with a high crown, just to the right of the *Warrior*
and in *Illus. 2,* immediately to the right of the *Scholar's Screen*) Although mythological references in Freud's writings are almost ex-
clusively Classical and not to Egyptian stories such as the legend of
Osiris, we might infer from the prominent presence on Freud's desk
of statues of *Osiris,* his wife *Isis suckling Horus,* and underworld at-
tendant the *Baboon of Thoth* that the story may have interested the
discoverer of the unconscious mind.[25] The complex legend tells of
a terrestrial king with a devoted wife who was murdered by his
brother and then became ruler of the world of the dead, located "under" the world of the living. As patron of writing and scribe of the
gods, Thoth had charge of the "Weighing of the Heart" ceremony

Illustration 3.   Statuette of God Imhotep, Egyptian, Late Period, 716-332 B.C., bronze, height 4³/₄ inches. Freud Museum, London.

conducted in the underworld after death to determine the virtue and truthfulness of the deceased. The Baboon of Thoth sat atop the scale, from which vantange point he could announce to Osiris whether or not the deceased was "true of voice." The idea of a shadowy underworld filled with "spirits" or "life forces" from the past which are judged as to their truthfulness, recalls Freud's concept of the unconscious mind as revealed in the analytic session.

The healing power of dreams was represented on Freud's desk by the seated bronze *Imhotep* (*Illus. 3*), the Egyptian architect and sage, who the Greeks later identified with Asklepios, the god of medicine. Freud recalls in *The Interpretation of Dreams* that in classical times a patient would go to a temple of Asklepios in search of recovery, where he would sleep and dream the remedies of his illness "either in their natural form or in symbols and pictures which would afterwards be interpreted by the priests." (*SE*, vol. 4, p. 34n)

This examination of Freud's desk—both the arrangement of an "audience" and the identity of several specific figures—suggests that one driving force behind Freud's multidetermined passion to collect antiquities was his need for colleagues during his early years of professional isolation and his lifelong struggle for the acceptance of his theories. Freud's most immediate audience was not hostile, narrow-minded and anti-Semitic; it was neither the Viennese medical community, nor the learned societies. Rather, protected by warriors, Freud wrote in the company of scholars and a goddess of wisdom, a figure who could see in more than one direction, a patron of all things intellectual who was also a judge of who was "true of voice," a ruler of the underworld, and a god of medicine who healed through the interpretation of dreams. The father of psychoanalysis—that explorer who discovered the unconscious mind and childhood sexuality—surrounded himself with manifestations of his own passion to possess.

2

The Pagan Freud

Peter Loewenberg

I

Freud had a Jewish cultural identity and was a cultural pagan. Of course, both sides of the statement are true. While there is a voluminous secondary literature on Freud's Jewish identity, there is little on his paganism.[1] It is this Hellenic-Roman aspect of Freud's person and legacy which this essay explores. I wish to engage the culturally non-Hebraic, and indeed theologically specifically anti-Mosaic, portion of Freud's interest, commitment, and esthetic emotional investment. Freud worshiped the culture of antiquity and shared its anti-Judeo-Christian values.

Freud was a pagan in the etymological sense that the term *paganus* was applied by the early Christian Church to those who followed Greek, Roman, and other faiths and refused to accept the only true God. As the eleventh edition of the *Encyclopaedia Britannica* (1911) put it:

> A special significance attaches to the word when applied to one who adopts that attitude of cultured indifference to, or negation of, the various theistic systems of religion which was taken by so

This essay is dedicated to my friends, Robert and Geraldine Dallek. I wish to acknowledge the helpful consultations of David Lee, Rena Freedman, Fredrick Redlich, Arnold and Ora Band in its preparation.

many of the educated and aristocratic classes in the ancient Hellenic and Roman world.[2]

Freud was a Hellenic pagan in four main dimensions of his personality: 1) Most importantly in his oedipal triumph over his poor Jewish merchant father; 2) his admiration and identification with the aesthetics of what he viewed as a superior culture, and the geography of Mediterranean antiquity; 3) his enlightened plea for a tolerant non-judgmental sexual morality; 4) his personal philosophy of stoicism and in the manner in which he faced his death.

Not one of the artifacts in the sumptuous 1989 publication of Freud's personal collection of antiquities was Judaic.[3] Peter Gay in the "Introduction" to the volume writes of Freud:

> His antiquities, many of them from countries he had never visited and many of them originating in the region from which his remote ancestors had come, spoke to him of his Jewishness.[4]

I would argue precisely the converse—that the substantial collection of classical antiquities Freud assembled were, at the least, non-Judaic, explicitly anti-Biblical, tributes to paganism. The observance of the Mosaic interdiction against graven images insured that with the exception of ritual Torah decorations, candelabra, and kiddush cups, religious artifacts which approximated human or animal figures did not exist in post-Mosaic Judaism. Where Jewish artifacts or figures, such as lions, did appear it was not for cultic purposes. The figures Freud collected were pagan cultic and totemic figures. As Ellen Handler Spitz correctly points out:

> In emphasizing that Freud elected for himself an intellectual heritage different from that of his ancestors, it seems hardly necessary to point out that none of his cherished ancient objects is in any sense Jewish and that Jewish rituals and observance were anathema to him.[5]

I wish to suggest that the antiquities, Hellenic, Roman, and Egyptian, which Freud collected were manifest symbols of his tribute to paganism. He, of course, did not worship them, but tribute he did bring. He undertook pilgrimages to the sites of ancient glory in Athens and Rome. He wrote to Stefan Zweig in 1931:

> Despite my much vaunted frugality I have sacrificed a great deal for my collection of Greek, Roman and Egyptian antiquities, have actually read more archaeology than psychology, and . . . before the war and once after its end I felt compelled to spend every year at least several days or weeks in Rome.[6]

Occasionally Freud brought further sacrifice by unconsciously destroying a beloved cult figure from his collection in order to expiate a hostile act, or a fantasied aggression, or to elicit a desired gift. Freud not only prided himself on his collection of antiquities, but also on his facility in not breaking them. Although he denied any special dexterity, he was proud of his skill in moving among his clutter of objects. He had no doubt that each of the rare breakages fulfilled an unconscious purpose. Each case of an "accident" with his antiquities was cherished and fondled as a relic from an archeological excavation. It was a symptomatic act to be treasured, interpreted, and worked through. He tells us in *The Psychopathology of Everyday Life* (1901):

> It is very rare for me to break anything. I am not particularly dexterous but a result of the anatomical integrity of my nerve-muscle apparatus is that there are clearly no grounds for my making clumsy movements of this kind, with their unwelcome consequences. I cannot therefore recall any object in my house that I have ever broken. Shortage of space in my study has often forced me to handle a number of pottery and stone antiquities (of which I have a small collection) in the most uncomfortable positions, so that onlookers have expressed anxiety that I should knock something down and break it. That however has never happened. Why then did I once dash the marble cover of my plain inkpot to the ground so that it broke?
>
> My inkstand is made out of a flat piece of Untersberg marble which is hollowed out to receive the glass inkpot; and the inkpot has a cover with a knob made of the same stone. Behind this

inkstand there is a ring of bronze statuettes and terra cotta figures. I sat down at the desk to write, and then moved the hand
that was holding the pen-holder forward in a remarkably clumsy
way, sweeping on to the floor the inkpot cover which was lying on
the desk at the time.

The explanation was not hard to find. Some hours before, my sister had been in the room to inspect some new acquisitions. She
admired them very much, and then remarked: 'Your writing table
looks really attractive now; only the inkstand doesn't match. You
must get a nicer one.' I went out with my sister and did not return
for some hours. But when I did I carried out, so it seems, the ex-
ecution of the condemned inkstand. Did I perhaps conclude from
my sister's remark that she intended to make me a present of a
nicer inkstand on the next festive occasion, and did I smash the
unlovely one so as to force her to carry out the intention she
had hinted at? If that is so, my sweeping movement was only
apparently clumsy; in reality it was exceedingly adroit and well-
directed, and understood how to avoid damaging any of the more
precious objects that stood around.[7]

This breaking was unconsciously instrumental, even manipulative,
in its purpose.

The example Freud gives of breaking "a beautiful little marble
Venus" as a propitiation to appease the Gods and render them fa-
vorable belongs in the category of magical thinking:

One morning, for example, when I was passing through a room
in my dressing gown with straw slippers on my feet, I yielded to
a sudden impulse and hurled one of my slippers from my foot at
the wall, causing a beautiful little marble Venus to fall down from
its bracket. As it broke into pieces, I quoted quite unmoved these
lines from Busch:

> 'Ach! die Venus ist perdu"—
> Klickeradoms!—von Medici!'
> Oh! the Venus! Lost is she!—
> Klickeradoms!—of Medici!

This wild conduct and my calm acceptance of the damage are to
be explained in terms of the situation at the time. One of my fam-

ily was gravely ill, and secretly I had already given up hope of her recovery. That morning I had learned that there had been a great improvement, and I know I had said to myself: 'So she's going to live after all.' My attack of destructive fury served therefore to express a feeling of gratitude to fate and allowed me to perform a 'sacrificial act'—rather as if I had made a vow to sacrifice something or other as a thank-offering if she recovered her health! The choice of the Venus of Medici for this sacrifice was clearly only a gallant act of homage towards the convalescent; but even now it is a mystery to me how I made up my mind so quickly, aimed so accurately and avoided hitting anything else among the objects so close to it.[8]

The final example Freud gives us is one of expiation for aggression.

I had once seen fit to reproach a loyal and deserving friend on no other grounds than the interpretation I placed on certain indications coming from his unconscious. He was offended and wrote me a letter asking me not to treat my friends psycho-analytically. I had to admit he was in the right, and wrote him a reply to pacify him. While I was writing this letter I had in front of me my latest acquisition, a handsome glazed Egyptian figure. I broke it in the way I have described, and then immediately realized that I had caused this mischief in order to avert a greater one. Luckily it was possible to cement both of them together—the friendship as well as the figure—so that the break would not be noticed.[9]

Freud describes this as "a propitiatory sacrifice to avert evil." He broke his beloved Egyptian idol because of his hostility and tactlessness in offering an unsolicited interpretation to a friend. The sacrifice of his newest antiquity was in expiation for inappropriate and unfair aggression.[10]

II

Freud's symbolic codes for the conceptualization of unconscious structures and conflicts were derived from Greek mythology: Narcissus, Oedipus, Laius, Jocasta, Kronos, Zeus, Juno, Alecto,

Iphigenia, the Three Fates, Medusa, Aeneas, and Ulysses. All his life he was indebted to his classical Gymnasium education for opening to him the world of antiquity.

In Freud's essay for the *Festschrift* of the Gymnasium he attended between the ages of nine and seventeen (1865–1873), he pays homage to the schoolmasters who imparted to him the humanistic spirit, the classical languages, and Greek and Roman history, which were:

> My first glimpses of an extinct civilization which in my case was to bring me as much consolation as anything else in the struggles of life.[11]

Clearly Freud is here referring to the Greco-Roman world of pagan antiquity, not to his father's extinct civilization of the Old Testament. As if to reaffirm the rejection of his father and his Hebraic world in the new adherence to Hellenic antiquity, Freud goes on in the same essay to explicate the Oedipal dynamics of a son who rejects, criticizes, and excels over his father:

> In the second half of childhood a change sets in the boy's relation to his father—a change whose importance cannot be exaggerated. From his nursery the boy begins to cast his eyes upon the world outside. And he cannot fail now to make discoveries which undermine his original high opinion of his father and which expedite his detachment from his first ideal. He finds that his father is no longer the mightiest, wisest and richest of beings; he grows dissatisfied with him, he learns to criticize him and to estimate his place in society; and then, as a rule, he makes him pay heavily for the disappointment that has been caused by him.[12]

This motif came to its fullest expression over two decades later, toward the end of his life, when Freud returned to the twin themes of the glory of ancient Attica, as he had learned it in the humanistic Gymnasium, and how this represents a triumph over his impoverished wool merchant father who did not have the benefit of a classical education. This further piece of Oedipal self-analysis, written in Freud's eighty-first year, is in the form of a letter of congratulations to Romain Rolland on his seventieth birthday. The analytic task is to understand a depression he and his brother felt in 1904 in Trieste upon learning that a long cherished dream of at last visiting Athens and viewing the Acropolis would be realized, and to analyze the sensation of de-realization which Freud experienced standing on the Acropolis, the thought: "So all this really *does* exist, just as we learnt at school!" He had a "momentary feeling: '*What I see here is not real.*'" These two phenomena—the depression in Trieste and the derealization on the Acropolis—were intimately related. The emotional connection is surpassing his father, excelling over him, travelling further than he did, and cherishing sights and evocations of antiquity for which his father would have had no appreciation. Freud's analysis is:

> A sense of guilt was attached to the satisfaction in having gone such a long way: there was something about it that was wrong, that from earliest times had been forbidden. It was something to do with a child's criticism of his father, with the undervaluation which took the place of the overvaluation of earlier childhood. It seems as though the essence of success was to have got further than one's father, and as though to excel one's father was still something forbidden. . . . The very theme of Athens and the Acropolis in itself contained evidence of the son's superiority. Our father had been in business, he had had no secondary education, and Athens could not have meant much to him. Thus what interfered with our enjoyment of the journey to Athens was a feeling of *filial piety.*[13]

The eighty-year old Freud was still working through his oedipal struggle with his father who had died forty years earlier.

III

Freud's dreams and associations bear direct testimony to his piety to classical Greece and Rome. Freud offered us what he called "a series of dreams which are based upon a longing to visit Rome." His first example is:

> I was looking out of a railway-carriage window at the Tiber and the Ponte Sant' Angelo. The train began to move off, and it

occurred to me that I had not so much as set foot in the city. The view that I had seen in my dream was taken from a well-known engraving which I had fleetingly noticed the day before in the sitting-room of one of my patients. Another time someone led me to the top of a hill and showed me Rome half-shrouded in mist; it was so far away that I was surprised at my view of it being so clear. There was more in the content of this dream than I feel prepared to detail; but the theme of 'the promised land [*das gelobte Land*] seen from afar' was obvious in it.[14]

Freud often spoke of the work of psychoanalysis in the metaphor of archeological excavation: "It is as if Schliemann had dug up another Troy...."[15] The classic text he left us, *The Interpretation of Dreams*, is also in his lifetime a living, multi-layered text, requiring careful exfoliation of Freud's accretions and emendations to the various editions. To the Castel Sant' Angelo dream we find added in 1909:

BRIDGE AND CASTLE OF ST. ANGELO.

"I discovered long since that it only needs a little courage to fulfill wishes which till then have been regarded as unattainable," and in 1925 the further association: "and [I] thereafter became a fervent pilgrim to Rome."[16]

The manifest content of this dream includes specific Christian, Classical, Jewish, and secular scientific associations as well as day residue with an Oedipal meaning. The day residue was an engraving he viewed in the salon of a patient the previous day. Freud specifically places the social locus of this Roman cultural artifact in the genteel environment of the home of his patient, who is a member of the *Bildungsburgertum,* the educated Viennese upper middle class. Freud did not see this engraving in his childhood home. By contrast, when Goethe travelled to Rome, he thought of the pictures in his father's entrance hall.

> Now I see in life all the dreams of my youth. The first engravings I recall—my father hung the views of Rome in an antechamber—I now see in reality. And everything which I have known for a long time in paintings and drawings, engravings and woodcuts, in plaster and cork, now stands assembled before me; wherever I go I find an acquaintance in a new world.[17]

Freud's self-description, *Rompilger,* is a specifically Roman Catholic usage, acknowledging the Christian Rome. The Castel Sant' Angelo was the fortress of the Popes connected to the Vatican by a tunnel.[18] Here the Popes took refuge from enemies, as when Rome was sacked by the armies of Charles V in 1527.

Behind the Christian Rome stands the pagan classical Rome. The Ponte Sant' Angelo [*Engelsbrucke*] was built by Hadrian in 135 A.D. and adorned with statues by Bernini in the seventeenth century. The castle was originally built by Hadrian as his mausoleum. The Emperor Hadrian was cursed by the Jews for the Hadrianic persecutions which included forbidding the observance of the Sabbath and the rite of circumcision, banning the teaching of the Torah and the maintenance of religious organization. Hadrian made Jerusalem a pagan city with the figure of a boar over its gate. No Jew was allowed to set foot in the city.

Freud recalls and associates to the famous lines of the Old Testament from the final pages of the book of *Deuteronomy,* when God spoke to Moses on Mount Nebo overlooking the land of Canaan:

> You may view the land from a distance, but you shall not enter it. *Deuteronomy,* 33:52.

> And the Lord said to him; this is the land of which I swore to Abraham, Isaac, and Jacob, "I will give it to your offspring." I have let you see it with your own eyes, but you shall not cross there. *Deuteronomy,* 34:4.

These final passages of the *Torah* are known to all observant Jews, not only because they include God's covenant with Moses granting the children of Israel the promised land, but also because these verses are read on the last day of the Jewish year. As this reading is finished religious Jews immediately commence reading the first lines of the book of *Genesis,* to sustain the continuity of the learning of the Holy Writ.

When Freud wrote:

> The motif of "the Holy Land seen from afar" is easy to recognize in it.

> *Das Motiv, "das gelobte Land von ferne sehen," ist darin leicht zu erkennen.*

he was placing himself toward Rome as Moses was to Israel, he was only permitted to view the promised land from afar. He dreamt of looking at, but of being unable to reach, the tomb of a Roman Emperor which had become a symbol of the papacy.

It is important that Freud dreamed of the bridge rather than the castle, although the two are contiguous. His view in the dream is across the bridge (*Brücke*), evoking the name of his admired Prussian professor of neurophysiology in whose laboratory he worked for six years of critical growth, who represented Freud's scientific ideal of the rigorous, positivist, precise, nineteenth century scientist. Ernst Brücke was his adored mentor who proposed and supported him for the study fellowship to Paris. Freud named his third son, Ernst (b. 1892) after his beloved teacher. Freud's associations to Brücke are analyzed in the "Non Vixit" dream in the *Interpretation of Dreams*. The emotional setting was an infraction and a reprimand:

> At the time I have in mind I had been a demonstrator at the Physiological Institute and was due to start work early in the morning. It came back to Brücke's ears that I sometimes reached the students' laboratory late. One morning he turned up punctually at the hour of opening and awaited my arrival. His words were spare and to the point. But it was not the words that mattered. What overwhelmed me were the terrifying blue eyes with which he looked at me and before which I shank. . . . Any one who can remember the great master's eyes, which retained their wonderful beauty even in his old age, and who has ever seen him in anger, will find it easy to identify with the young sinner's emotions.[19]

Freud dreamt of the Ponte Sant' Angelo before having visited Rome. When he did eventually reach Rome in 1901, he was "overwhelmed" at what he described to Fliess as "the fulfillment of a long cherished wish," which was "a high point of my life." He contrasted the pagan Rome, to which he felt reverence, with the Christian Rome with its false promise of eternal salvation:

> I could have worshiped [*anbeten*] the abased and mutilated remnant of the Temple of Minerva near the forum of Nerva, I found I could not freely enjoy the second [the medieval, Christian] Rome; the atmosphere troubled me. I found it difficult to tolerate the lie concerning man's redemption, which raises its head to high heaven—for I could not cast off the thought of my own misery and all the other misery I know about.

> I found the third, the Italian, Rome full of promise and likable.

>> I was frugal in my pleasures, though, and did not try to see everything in twelve days. I not only bribed the Trevi [fountain], as everyone does, I also—and I invented this

myself—dipped my hand in the Bocca della Verità at Santa Maria Cosmedin and vowed to return.[20]

Freud was captivated by the serene beauty of the sites of classic antiquity. He found peace and healing there and he prescribed a visit to the glories of *Magna Graecia* as a "cure" for a conversion symptom. The patient was the young Viennese conductor Bruno Walter in 1906. The symptom was a cramping paralysis with "rheumatic-neuralgic pain"

> . . . so violent that I could no longer use my right arm for conducting or piano playing. I went from one prominent doctor to another. Each one confirmed the presence of psychogenic elements in my malady. I submitted to any number of treatments, from mudbaths to magnetism, and finally decided to call on Professor Sigmund Freud, resigned to submit to months of soul searching. The consultation took a course I had not foreseen. Instead of questioning me about sexual aberrations in infancy, as my layman's ignorance had led me to expect, Freud examined my arm briefly. I told him my story, feeling certain that he would be professionally interested in a possible connection between my actual physical affliction and a wrong I had suffered more than a year before. Instead, he asked me if I had ever been to Sicily. When I replied that I had not, he said that it was very beautiful and interesting and more Greek than Greece itself. In short, I was to leave that very evening, forget all about my arm and the Opera, and do nothing for a few weeks but use my eyes. I did as I was told. Fortified with all the available literature about Sicily, I took an evening train for Genoa. . . . Milan and Venice were the only Italian beauty spots thus far known to me. I had purposely chosen the sea route, because I would have considered it unbearable, if not sinful, to rush in a train through cities like Florence and Rome just to get to Sicily quickly enough and be able to use for the intended purpose what little time my finances permitted me. . . . I was anxious to get to Sicily, and I took the regular steamer to Palermo the following evening. The boat was small, the seas were high, and I was disgracefully seasick, but I felt richly compensated by the splendid entrance into the port of Palermo and the sight of Monte Pellegrino in the morning air.

Mindful of Freud's instructions, I endeavored not to think of my afflication. In this I was aided by the powerful and exciting effect of my first meeting with Hellenism, which burst upon my eye and soul from every side. I was deeply impressed by the Greek theater in Taormina, the boatride on the Anapo beneath the papyrus shrubs, and the temples of Girgenti. But all these individual sights were outshone by the magnificient landscape with its grandiosely shaped mountains, the sublime solitude surrounding Syracuse, the rivers, the fields, and the nobly shaped bays. This, indeed, seemed an ideal scenery for Goethe's *Walpurgisnacht*. Thoughts of a tempestuous past, of the monuments commemorating it, and of nature that seemed to bear its imprint agitated me for weeks and made me forget the present and my troubles. In the end, my soul and mind were greatly benefited by the additional knowledge I had gained of Hellenism, but not my arm.[21]

Although Freud cherished his collection of pagan artifacts, he had no tolerance for holy places or sacred sites in the contemporary practice of religion. An unpublished letter written sixty years ago regarding the holy places in Jerusalem expresses Freud's ambivalence toward Zionism and the worship of sacred sites. In 1929 Arab riots in Palestine opposed the Zionist settlement and particularly Jewish right of access to the Wailing Wall, the remnant of the foundation of the Second Temple considered holy by orthodox Jews. The Palestine Foundation Fund (*Keren Hajessod*) solicited letters around the world from prominent Jews, including Sigmund Freud, seeking support of the right of Jews to access to the Wall.

Freud's answer to Keren Hajessod, Vienna, was:

> I cannot do what you wish. I am unable to overcome my aversion to burdening the public with my name and even the present critical time does not seem to me to warrant it. Whoever wants to influence the masses must give them something rousing and inflammatory and my sober judgement of Zionism does not permit this. I certainly sympathize with its goals, am proud of our University in Jerusalem and am delighted with our settlements' prosperity. But, on the other hand, I do not think that Palestine could ever become a Jewish state, nor that the Christian and

Islamic worlds would ever be prepared to have their holy places under Jewish control. It would have seemed more sensible to me to establish a Jewish homeland on a less historically burdened land. But I know that such a rational viewpoint would never have gained the enthusiasm of the masses and the financial support of the wealthy. I concede with sorrow that the unrealistic fanaticism of our people is in part to be blamed for the awakening of Arab distrust. I have no sympathy at all for the misdirected piety which transforms a piece of Herod's wall into a national relic thereby challenging the feelings of the natives.

Now judge for yourself whether I, with such a critical position, am the right person to stand forth to comfort a people deluded by unjustified hope.[22]

The cover letter from Vienna to Jerusalem was equally interesting and explains why this letter of Freud's and its glosses remained unpublished for over four decades.[23] It is from Dr. Chaim Koffler of the Keren Hajessod, Vienna, to Dr. Abraham Schwadron, a right wing Zionist who had a famous autograph collection in the Jewish National and University Library, Jerusalem. It reads:

The letter of Freud, with all its genuineness and warmth for us, is not propitious. And since there are no secrets in Palestine, the letter will certainly find its way out of the autograph collection of the University Library into the public eye. If I cannot be of service to the Keren Hajessod, I at least feel myself bound not to do damage. Should you wish to personally see the handwriting, then to return it to me, I will send the handwriting to you via a tourist, Dr. Manka Spiegel, who is travelling to Palestine, and who will later return the letter to me.

This letter bears a fascinating handwritten Hebrew postscript in which Schwadron responds to Koffler:

It is true that in Palestine there are no secrets . . . but I have not become naturalized. . . . The collection is without help as it was . . . it is in *splendid isolation* [original in English transliterated in Hebrew characters] . . . it has no contact with the public,

except for special things . . . it contains many manuscripts
and pictures from all points of view: not to be shown and not to
be handed over to anyone and as for me . . . a non-Zionist, that is
to say precise and exact . . . a sense of responsibility . . . I "order
you like the celestial messengers" [*Daniel* 4:14] to hurry . . . I
promise you . . . in the name of the library that "no human eye
shall see it" [*Job* 7:8] . . .

> With full responsibility . . . [24]

Following this Biblical command, Freud's letter was sent to
Jerusalem and the promise of non-publication was kept. Although
Freud was wrong about his prediction—the Jewish state does exist—as he was often wrong about other political assessments, such
as that the Austro Fascists would restrain the Nazis, sadly his interpretation about the conflict over the holy sites has as much reso-
nance today as it did over sixty years ago. Freud was not a political
Zionist and he did not believe in sanctifying stones.

Freud's non-Judeo-Christian, indeed anti-Old and New Testament, position on sexual morality is most eloquently stated when
he invokes the Greeks as a superior and more tolerant sexual and
cultural ideal. For example, in the "Dora" case, Freud admonishes:

We must learn to speak without indignation of what we call the
sexual perversions—instances in which the sexual function has
extended its limits in respect either to the part of the body concerned or to the sexual object chosen. The uncertainty in regard
to the boundaries of what is to be called normal sexual life, when
we take different races and different epochs into account, should
in itself be enough to cool the zealot's ardour. We surely ought
not to forget that the perversion which is the most repellent to us,
the sensual love of a man for a man, was not only tolerated by a
people so far our superiors in cultivation as were the Greeks [*so
sehr kulturüberlegenen Volke wie den Griechen*], but was actually entrusted by them with important social functions. The sexual life of each one of us extends to a slight degree—now in this
direction, now in that—beyond the narrow lines imposed as the
standard of normality. The perversions are neither bestial nor de-
generate in the emotional sense of the word.[25]

In Freud's parallel text of psychodynamic theory which was published the same year as the "Dora" case, he stresses the distinction between inverts and degenerates and argues:

> Account must be taken of the fact that inversion was a frequent phenomenon—one might almost say an institution charged with important functions—among the peoples of antiquity at the height of their civilization.[26]

Freud notes with approval the turn from ethnocentric marginalization of homosexuals to an historical and ethnographic relativism and again invokes the case of pagan Hellas and Rome:

> The pathological approach to the study of inversion has been displaced by the anthropological. The merit for bringing about this change is due to Bloch (1902–3), who has also laid stress on the occurrence of inversion among the civilizations of antiquity.[27]

A third of a century later, when writing to an American mother, Freud offered her the Stoic comfort of historical antiquity:

> I gather from your letter that your son is a homosexual. I am most impressed by the fact that you do not mention this term yourself in your information about him. May I question you why you avoid it? Homosexuality is assuredly no advantage, but it is nothing to be ashamed of, no vice, no degradation; it cannot be classified as an illness; we consider it to be a variation of the sexual function, produced by a certain arrest of sexual development. Many highly respectable individuals of ancient and modern times have been homosexuals, several of the greatest men among them. (Plato, Michelangelo, Leonardo da Vinci, etc.) It is a great injustice to persecute homosexuality as a crime—and a cruelty, too.[28]

V

For the stratum of Austrian secular Jewish intelligensia of the late nineteenth century to which Freud belonged the culture of reference was Hellenic-Roman. The statue of Athena, symbolizing the wisdom of rational law, stands before the classic Greek Parliament building on Vienna's Ringstrasse.[29]

Freud was a philosophical Stoic and lived his personal life by that creed learned from Seneca and Epictetus in his humanistic Gymnasium. The Stoics taught the world the conception of the weakness and misery of men, individually and in society. They sought in Stoic philosophy a refuge against the vicissitudes of fortune which they beheld daily and maintained the essential dignity and internal freedom of every human being. Their attitude was tolerant of suicide as a "way out" of incurable discomforts including the infirmity of old age.[30] The essence of Stoic philosophy as Freud learned it and practiced it was to accept the inevitable with dignity and resolution.

In his personal life, his psychotherapeutic stance, and in his world view, Freud was submissive to natural law and the cruelties of fate, such as the death of a beloved grandson, or the malignancy which tormented him for the last sixteen years of his life and which eventually killed him. Thus, in 1895 he tells patients who want miracles:

> No doubt fate would find it easier than I do to relieve you of your illness. But you will be able to convince yourself that much will be gained if we succeed in transforming your hysterical misery into common unhappiness. With a mental life that has been restored to health you will be better armed against that unhappiness.[31]

This is Freud, the Stoic, speaking. When, over three decades later, he was to write of "the great necessities of Fate, against which there is no help [which we must] learn to endure with resignation,"[32] we hear the teachings of the Stoics which Freud had made his personal philosophy of life and death.

The final test for any man who is a Stoic is the way he dies. We have the remarkable account of the last ten years of Freud's life and his ordeal with cancer from Max Schur, his last personal physician. Freud faced his malignancy with full cognizance of the certainty of

his death. In Freud's experience, as was generally true in the pre-
antibiotic era, death was life's companion. He lived in the presence
of death from childhood. He lost an infant brother; in 1914 his beloved half-brother Emmanuel was killed in a railway accident; others close to him who died were his friends Ernst von Fleishl-
Marxow and Anton von Freund; his daughter Sophie in 1920, when
she was only 26, then her four-year old son Heinele in 1923.

Meeting with death is never without denial and ambivalence,
both by the patient and his caretakers. In Freud's case this ambivalence was dramatic in his original suspicions of cancer and his in-
action and the reassurances and denials from his physician and
inner circle. In the spring of 1923 he detected a growth on his right
jaw and palate. For two months he did not mention it to a family
member, physician, friend, or take steps to have the growth examined.[33] When he showed it to his physician, Felix Deutsch, he did so
with the comment, "Be prepared to see something you won't like."
Upon examination, said Deutsch, "At the very first glance, I had no
doubt that it was an advanced cancer."[34]

Freud chose Marcus Hajek to operate on him, a man who "was
generally known to be a somewhat mediocre surgeon" and about
whom he had misgivings because he was aware of Hajek's ambivalence toward him.[35] This was a decision that nearly cost Freud his
life. He was not properly cared for nor hospitalized, and he almost
bled to death. The surgeon did not take the usual precautions
against the shrinking of the scar, thereby causing Freud hardship
for the rest of his life.[36] Hajek did not tell Freud that he had cancer.
Both Deutsch and Freud's "Committee," his most trusted disciples,
also withheld from him the diagnosis of cancer and the need for
a second major operation. Years later, when Ernest Jones told him
of the Committee's deception, Freud "with blazing eyes . . . asked
'*Mit welchem Recht?*'"[37] He was full of reproach towards Deutsch
because the accurate diagnosis was withheld from him and he was
deceived. Very likely, had Freud been confronted with the true
diagnosis, he would not have been so casual about his first sur-
gery, agreeing to go to an outpatient clinic with no hospital room,
bed, or proper nursing care. Freud wrote to Deutsch invoking his
Stoic ideal:

I could always adapt myself to any kind of reality, even endure an uncertainty due to a reality—but being left alone with my subjective insecurity, without the fulcrum or pillar of the *ananke,* the inexorable, unavoidable necessity, I had to fall prey to the miserable cowardice of a human being and had to become an unworthy spectacle for others.[38]

During the next sixteen years Freud underwent thirty-three operations of the mouth. As ever greater areas of the jaw, palate and cheek were removed in increasingly radical operations, he had to learn to live with a huge prosthesis which he termed "the monster." Felix Deutsch notes that Freud "never complained about his misfortune to me; in these years he simply treated the neoplasm as an uninvited, unwelcome intruder whom one should not mind more than necessary."[39]

In 1928, Freud took a new physician, Max Schur. He did so under two conditions, one that he always be told the truth, and second, "that when the time comes, you won't let me suffer unnecessarily."[40] When, in September 1939, Freud asked Schur to redeem his promise, Schur gave him two centigrams of morphine which he repeated after twelve hours. Freud did not wake up again.[41]

Freud showed no sign of complaint or irritability. His stoic resignation to fate and his acceptance of unalterable reality never wavered nor faltered. With the exception of an occasional aspirin, he took no drugs until the very end so that he could think clearly. He continued his psychoanalytic work until July 1939. He died on September 23, a Stoic pagan to the end, believing in life. Death was the necessary outcome of life. Death is natural, undeniable, and unavoidable. Freud was unflinching about what he termed:

one of the most aggravating features of our modern medicine. The art of deceiving a sick person is not exactly highly necessary. But what has the individual come to, how negligible must be the influence of the religion of science, which is supposed to have taken the place of the old religion, if one no longer dares to disclose that it is this or that man's turn to die?. . . . I hope that when my time comes, I shall find someone who will treat me with greater respect and tell me when to be ready.

Freud unconsciously altered Shakespeare's *Henry IV* (Act V, Scene I) where Prince Hal tells Falstaff: "Why, Thou owest God a death" to "You owe Nature a death" (*"Du bist der Natur einen Tod schuldig."*) To this letter he adds the postscript: "I am deep in Burckhardt's *History of Greek Civilization.*"[42]

Freud's attitude toward death: forthright, without sentimentality or self-pity, but with a full consciousness of reality, represents the best of what Freud means for man's attitude toward himself: stoic acceptance. This life is all there is and there is little you can do about it. Man must die and that fact should not be obviated or denied. We must live with that realization and die, if possible, with a minimum of suffering and without illusions. This is what the Stoic pagan Freud had to offer—no panacea, utopia, or life after death—as he said in the beginning of his career as a psychoanalyst almost half a century earlier, all he could offer was the transformation of neurotic misery into the ability to cope with the "common unhappiness" which is our lot as humans.

3

Signs of the Fathers: Freud's Collection of Antiquities

Juliet Flower MacCannell

I. The Ethical Hypothesis of Freudian and Lacanian Theories: Enjoyment, the Object and the Subject

1. An Ethic of Jouissance

In psychoanalytic theory, *hatred* of the other is more primitive than love, because the *other* is seen as being in competition for the object of enjoyment. If *you* do not enjoy consumption of the object, you believe that this is because someone else—the other—*is* enjoying it.[1]

2. Desire

Desire is the opposite of *enjoyment* (*jouissance*). It is the recognition that the other, too, lacks enjoyment of the object. Desire

---

This essay contributes to the question of the transmission of semiotic insight through art, especially everyday arts and crafts. It locates certain questions of the place of art objects in the ethics of postmodernism.

I use the theory of Jacques Lacan[2] on the problematic of enjoyment (*la jouissance*) to situate my analysis of Freud's private collection of antique art objects from diverse cultures of the ancient past. I will show that they reveal Freud's belief in the ethical necessity of sustaining the Father function [*speech and desire*] even when the beings who support the paternal function today (woman, the child, even animals) do not appear in the expected traditional form of "the father" (father of the family, leader, priest, etc.) One further objective of this paper is to begin to make a distinction between the Lacanian concept of the *object a* and the fetish on the basis of the dimension of enjoyment.

means that the other from whom you would demand satisfaction equally lacks fulfillment. This recognition appears through *the signifier*. The signifier is defined as what organizes the drift of language, but what is not (yet) anchored to a specific meaning (signified—or fulfillment of a drive): it only opens toward meaning and satisfaction.

3. Speech

Desire is thus the origin of *speech*—not *language* as a system, nor *discourse* as a set of signifying practices (speech *acts*)—but *speech,* the relation of signifier-to-signified, of lack-of-meaning to lack-of-meaning (and thus to lack-of-fulfillment). Speech is the product of the recognition that one must pass through the Desire of the other, through the signifier, to sustain the cultural dimension—meeting more than physical need through the other, while not ignoring those needs.[3]

4. The Signifier

The signifier is, therefore, the basic *social contract.* In psychoanalysis, this signifier is first seen as *the phallus,* simultaneously signifier of *lack* and *desire,* and recognizable as the *desire of the other.*

5. The Postmodern Problematic

The postmodern problematic, however, has to do with our new power, via consumer capitalism, to dispense with—to do without—desire. Consumer society promises both to do away with *competition for the object* ("there is plenty for everyone" in a "post-scarcity" world),[4] and, to eliminate the need for passing through the desire of the other—through speech and the signifier.

Our postmodern question is:

a) Can we dispense with the desire of the other, the signifier and speech, without a return of primitive envy simply because there is a profusion of "objects"?

or

b) Is it not, instead, necessary to retain the social contract (the need to go through the desire of the other), but not necessarily through the traditional, old-fashioned manifestation of the signifier—the phallus? It seems the phallus has been too inflated as a value to signify desire any longer in the postmodern world.

6. Object a

Lacan proposed, in addition to the phallus, the *object a*. This new term provides for the belief (current in postmodern life) that we can dispense with the desire of the other, since the *object a* is whatever appears to fill the lack in the other. It renders the other fantasmatically a site of *jouissance,* rather than of *desire.*

But it also permits us, on the contrary, to find a new opening of the social contract, a new kind of *signifier* for a postmodern desire.

For Lacan, the *object a* as a signifier is more primitive, a cruder structure, than the phallus. The breast, the gaze, the voice and faeces—*objects a*—are technically "pre-phallic" or pre-genital; but, like the phallus, they organize the partial drives. They are closer to the maternal than to the paternal body, but they are still separated from it, and therefore, they can signify *lack* and *loss of enjoyment*—our first gifts to the social contract. (When the *object a* fails to signify such lack in the maternal body, ascribing some invisible but fundamental enjoyment to her, then the *object a* loses ground to the *fetish,* the article of a faith that somewhere in the Other, It/She/the Thing—enjoys.)

The *object a,* then, is more adapted to the "neo-totemic" world of the postmodern[5] in that it takes us closer to the recognition of the primary ambivalence (hatred and love of the other through the object) necessary to re-establish the social contract as the recognition of lack-in-the-other. It is crucial, in the intercultural life we lead today, to overcome the assumption that the other is enjoying whenever we are not enjoying. Recent research by the Freudian school of Paris has shown this assumption to be at the root of racism.[6]

II. Freud's Collection of Antiquities and the Work of the *Object a*

Freud adumbrated Lacan's insights on these topics. Turning now to his collection of antiquities, my aim is to document Freud's appreciation for

1) the importance of desire and lack as a recognition of the loss of enjoyment for all speaking beings (Lacan calls them *parlêtres*)

2) the urgent need to reaffirm desire in the face of racism and genocide

3) the critical role played by the *objet a* as *objet d'art* (art-object) to construct an alternative signifier of desire for postmodernity.

For this critical ethical task of re-signifying desire, Freud's antiquities re-affirm the necessary link with "the Father," or the "paternal function," defined as the radical break with natural enjoyment and (therefore) its equation with speech (again, not discourse or language).

This is why, as I will now show, Freud took Charles Darwin (and most non-Western mythologies) very seriously, and demonstrated—long before Deleuze and Guattari suggested that we "become-animal,"—how our "father" was a monkey, a monkey who *decided to speak.*[7]

1. Animals

Freud's collection emphasizes our kinship with animals. It also reinserts "modern" life into the animal order, but it does not do so "scientifically," via biological classification. It does so at the level of culture. Much like his thesis in *Totem and Taboo,* Freud's collection confirms the "neo-totemic" character of contemporary, post-Kantian, ethics.[8] Equally, it criticizes implicitly both the *modernist fantasy* of liberating ourselves from all debts to the ancestor, and the *postmodern fantasy* that we no longer need to go through the signifier, the desire of the other.

These minor figurines may not at first appear significant, especially since Freud, like Lacan, explored more deeply "major" artists such as Leonardo, Michelangelo, Goethe, Shakespeare and Sophocles. But this collection of art objects was so valuable to Freud that he clung hysterically to them, making sure that he could carry them along when he was driven from Vienna by the Nazis. [They had virtually no economic or monetary value.] He honored them above his two old aunts, whom he left behind, deeming them too frail to be moved. Why? The answer is partly—but only partly—given by the fact that Freud felt that these objects literally allowed him to practice his profession: he ritually greeted them every day, before he entered his consulting room or sat down at his desk to write.

The complete set of art objects covered his desktop, and spilled over his consulting room on all sides in Vienna.

We have not yet approached the cause of Freud's compulsion for these objects.

2. The Collection as Index of Freud's Dialectic of Art and Civilization

When I first looked at the catalogue of Freud's antiquities[9] I was struck by something that had escaped me when I had seen the figures crowded into the plain little cabinet in the London house where Freud lived the last year of his life. That was the predominance of animal deities, half-men, half-animals, and half-women, in the collection Freud had been so anxious to wrest from the Nazi regime, and to accompany him in his flight from it. Freud's selection is further marked by the kindly, protective air these birds and monkeys, baboons and oxen have with respect to the humans with whom they consort and cohabit, often sharing the same body.

These vertically stacked, synchronic figures are totem-like: the animals occupy the uppermost positions above the human head, the "highest" point. (Later we see this reversed, with the human head above the animal body). In London, this collection lacks something of the aura of the Vienna rooms, because in Vienna, Freud placed them everywhere, not only in closed cabinets and on desks facing walls.

Anyone looking at Engelman's photos of Freud's Vienna apartment at Berggasse 19 (his living room and study communicated with his consulting room) has to see what the London arrangement fails to convey. Freud's desk top is not set for "business" alone, nor for the modern fantasy of writing in the absence of communication with the dead: in Vienna, his rooms teem with past life, ancestral figures; they have the energy and spirit of a veritable cult of the dead. . . .

Figure 1. Freud's study in Vienna. Photo by Edmund Engelman.

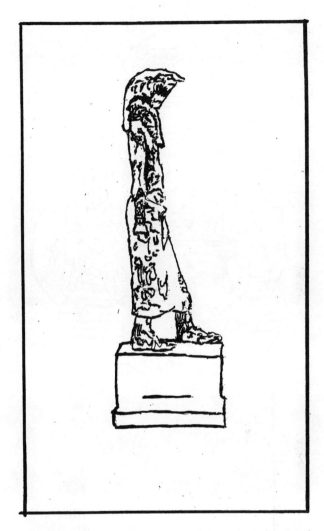

Figure 2. Falcon headed figure; 19th c. gessoed, painted
wood (forgery). Freud catalogue, p. 58. Line drawing by
Jason F. MacCannell.

Figure 3.   Head of King protected by Horus falcon; Egyptian, New kingdom
(18th dynasty); Stearite, original glazed; prob. reign of Menophis III 1390–
1353 BCE. Freud catalogue, p. 42. Line drawing by Jason F. MacCannell.

Figure 4. Isis suckling the infant Horus, with vulture-cow
headdress; Egyptian, Late Period, 126th dynasty; 624–525
BCE; Bronze 8 1/2 in. Freud catalogue, p. 52 Line drawing
by Jason F. MacCannell.

Figure 5.   Cabinet in London (cover photo; catalogue).
Line drawing by Jason F. MacCannell.

In Freud's apparent obligation to acknowledge, even propiti-
ate, this swarm of spirits, ghosts, predecessors, I discern the major
outlines of Freud's dialectic of art and civilization.

3. Monkey Business

About the time I first saw the catalogue of Freud's antiquities,
I was invited to be a guest at several of the 1990 Los Angeles Festival

Events where I (having recently translated Hélène Cixous's play about *Sihanouk*[10]) was anxious to see the traditional Cambodian Royal ballet, reconstituted from the remnants left after Pol Pot exterminated the classic dancers and artists. Here again, I came across more monkey business. The benign monkey-god, Hanuman, appeared as the hero of the centerpiece dance, the tale, taken from the *Ramayana,* of Sita's abduction. Hanuman's monkey band saves her when Rama's efforts prove fruitless against such refined mimetic evil.

Protective and faithful, courageous and upright, Hanuman embodies the best qualities of "man"—and yet he is not a man. Indeed, in contrast to the humans he serves (but who so depend on him) Hanuman is clearly inexpert in the arts of cultural refinement. While the royal personages are presented with exquisitely beautiful, but rather rigid behaviors and gestures. Hanuman and his troops are given to slightly awkward gestures; it is with some difficulty that these monkeys master the etiquette that permits them to communicate with the high-born humans—they lack "grace". On the other hand, the vilest crime (rape) in the tale is enabled by the villain's mimetic mastery of a perfect social grammar and by an exact imitation of his brother's voice.[11]

Thinking about this strange relation of the monkey to the moral order—a relation evident in Freud's collection—I remembered Freud's genuine admiration for Charles Darwin, the title of whose most provocative book constitutes an uncanny spatio-temporal dislocation: *The Descent of Man from Lower Animals.* While the term "descent," of course, means lineage, it also retains the spatial connotation of a journey downwards. Thus, if, according to Darwin, at the bottom of the journey towards manhood one finds the "lower animals" who are also at its source, we have the "highest" figure—either the child produced by the lineage or the primal father, as its source—in a strangely proximal relation to the *monkey.*

Monkeys abound in Freud's writings on civilization: the Scopes trial appears in a note (38) in *The Future of an Illusion*[12], for example. Monkeys also have a long relationship to "art." Consider this reproduction of Michelangelo's *Dying Slave* that Freud also kept on his desk: Note the monkey at the slave's feet. This monkey

Figure 6.   Freud with his copy of Michelangelo's *Dying Slave*. Freud catalogue, p. 20 Line drawing by Jason F. MacCannell.

is usually thought to symbolize, neo-Platonically, the brutal earthly passions that still ensnare the soul. Some critics, however, maintain—since there are monkeys in all the other statues planned for the monument to Pope Julius, the Pope who was a patron of the arts—that Michelangelo's monkeys simply stand for "art" as aping or mimesis.

The most important monkey-figure in Freud's collection is the marble Thoth, the (sometimes dog-faced) baboon god whose head,

Figure 7. *Dying Slave* (detail of monkey). Line drawing by
Jason F. MacCannell.

sporting a lunar disk, Freud patted every morning. Thoth is, like
Hanuman, linked to what we might call the ethical qualities—wisdom, learning, writing: but above all, intelligence about the human
heart. Thoth is the Egyptian god of death and writing.[13] It is he who
gives the human heart voice after death, weighing it on a balance
which reveals whether it has spoken true or not.[14]

Note how the lunar disk on the head of Thoth prefigures the
"phallic" (and solar) signifier in the form of the "hats" of the Amon-

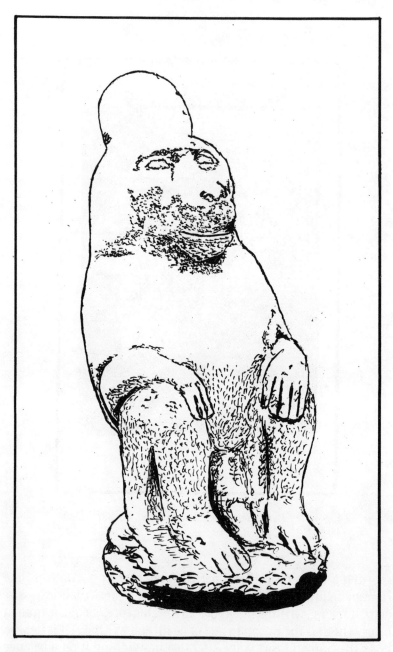

Figure 8. Thoth; Egyptian, Roman period, 30 BCE—AD 395, marble. Freud catalogue, p. 57. Line drawing by Jason F. MacCannell.

Figure 9.   Amon-re, sun-god, 716-332 B.C.E. Freud catalogue, p. 156. Line drawing by Jason F. MacCannell.

Re representations found in Freud's collection: Recall that, in
Freud's view, this sun-god was the precursor of monotheism and
Judeo-Christianity. But also note how the raising of the "symbolic
phallus" also begins to place the human head as superior to the animal body at the same period in history. It is as if, in this collection,
here Freud was making fun of, laughing at, the "idealization" of the
paternal function in the inflated figure of the phallus.

Figure 10.   Human-headed bird, Ptolemaic, 320 BCE, gessoed, painted wood. Freud catalogue, p. 72. Line drawing by
Jason F. MacCannell.

    If we recall that the difficult task, the labor of the signifier, is
to indicate both the loss of enjoyment of the object and anxiety[15] for
that enjoyment at the same time, then, by moving "the father figure" too far away from the "monkey-father" into an "idealized"
form, we lose the ethical requirement of *the signifier:* to recognize
the ambivalent pressure to *enjoy* (*the will to jouissance*) and the

Figure 11.   Sphinx amulet, Egyptian, late period, 716–332
BCE, faience. Freud catalogue, p. 50. Line drawing by Jason
F. MacCannell.

Figure 12.   Sphinx, South Italian, 5th–4th c. terra cotta. Freud catalogue, p. 93.

Figure 13.   Athena, figure of aggressive intellect, Roman,
1st or second century after a Greek original of the 5th century
BCE, bronze h. 4 1/2 in. Freud catalog. Line drawing by Jason
F. MacCannell.

equal "civil" pressure to forego *jouissance.* To choose either, at the expense of the other, is to lose humanity.

III. The Father Today: Art as Superego

The paternal has a protective as well as a prohibitive character for Freud and for Lacan. Whatever is literally *impossible—jouissance*—which is to say Real for the human, conscious being—is offered a Janus-face in the Superego, that of a Father who shelters us from the Real of Death and "untamed nature" by offering his verbal "No"—the origin of speech—in the place of what is a natural Law, an unchallengeable and uniform fate for us all. The paternal mode offers us what is impossible *as if it were an ethical choice.* We imagine we are free to disobey it. The Superego is itself also a reflection of the reality principle:

> external coercion gradually becomes internalized; for a special mental agency, man's super-ego, takes it over and includes it among its commandments. Every child presents this process of transformation to us; only by that means does it become a moral and social being. Such a strengthening of the super-ego is a most precious cultural asset in the psychological field. Those in whom it has taken place are turned from being opponents of civilization into being its vehicles. The greater their number is in a cultural unit the more secure is its culture and more it can dispense with external measures of coercion. (10–11)

The primal forms of hostility to collective civilization are incest and murder, especially cannibalism; these must be checked in the individual impulse if both the individual and the collective are to endure.

1. Animals and Fathers

Freud delineates the early figurations which have provided human beings with such regulative Superegos (dangerous and yet equally protective gods): *animal spirits* and *the father* himself, though he makes a distinction between them. In *Totem and Taboo,*

Figure 14. Cannibal figure, New Guinea from Milla, *Cannibal Caravan* (Preserved head is worked into lavish headdress).

the "first shape in which the protecting deity revealed itself to men" was "that of an animal"—solemnly prohibited from being consumed and eaten, yet ritually killed and eaten communally once a year. The totem animals are sacred and Freud's analysis links them to the earliest, most fundamental restrictions; totemism is the price paid for the conquest of and by the father, and the instituting of exogamy. (*F of I.*, 23)

Animal totems mark the limits on and of the human, but they do so dually: the things they prohibit (murder of the father; incest with the mother) are also the very misdeeds they symbolize yet do not state directly. What has become, through the acceptance of civilization, literally impossible for the conscious human being either to experience or to enjoy with full awareness (murder and incest), the animal deity at the summit of the totem pole conveys, albeit in a restrictive, moralized frame. It makes these elementary[16] prohibitions seem less *impossible* (in terms of reality) than *forbidden,* subject to a *taboo.* It is for this reason that the figures who represent these prohibitions purvey, qua animals, the idea of the *jouissance* that has been "deferred," held just out of the reach of civil man. [The Thoth Freud collected is, indeed, rather too polite in this respect; in most depictions he appears with an erection that reaches almost to his chin.]

In short, Freud purposely made the Father a figure of *menace* as well as of *benign protection* from the potential devastation of "mother" Nature, because of the specifically human requirement that we bear fully the weight of the ambivalent appeals of jouissance and of relinquishing that jouissance.[17]

2. Woman, Child, Savage, Artist and "Fathering"

If we flee from primal jouissance by hoping to give it over entirely to a "father," we destroy the possibility of "father" in the sense I am developing here. For giving up our need to recognize the pressure to enjoy and to defend ourselves against it, through speech, is to return again to in-fancy (the speechless condition), and to turn the "father" we seek into a complete full-bodied "mother." (This is what the idealist, daydreaming artist does, according to Freud.)[18]

The postmodern fantasy of dispensing with speech and the desire of the other ironically indexes a call to the "other" father—the grimace of the Real—again in the Monkey Father.

Within civilization, to the contrary of the desire to return to infancy, the child at play, the woman practicing her everyday household arts, the savage attempting to control nature through magic, the artist expressing primal wishes, are all effectively operating precisely the way the earliest "father" did: by remaining close to a level of *primal jouissance,* but *exchanging it for desire, for the signifier,* now recognizable in the outlines of the *object a.* Fantasy in play, as in art, the quotidian practical art object (weaving, pottery, cooking), the practice of magic, the labor of the artist—these are not "primitive" in the sense of unmediated primal *enjoyment,* but primitive in the sense that they remain close to the level of primary *desire,* the giving up, but constant reference to, primal enjoyments. Freud insisted (almost too clearly) on this in his essay on Fantasy: that the "first wish of the child," expressed in play, "is to become an adult."[19]

The child is not to be seen simply as the speechless infant of primary narcissism, but as someone hard at work *at play;* the woman must not be perceived as simply "nourishing mother" but as the maker of desire in her culinary variations on the breast-giving role: by boiling up "her water for chocolate" she is recognizing the desire of the other. The "primitive" shaman must not be deemed irrational and prescientific, but someone holding his people together through specialized narratives. Clearly Freud saw these as supporting the paternal function[20]—not the "idealized" father (*bon bourgeois père de famille*) of 19th–20th century bourgeois life. Kafka's father, whose *essen* is also always a *fressen,* is closer to what Freud has in mind. . . .

Freud insisted that the ideal ego—supposedly the "highest" self achieved by artificial civilization—needed to meet its own reality once again in the figure of the monkey father. After all, "idealization" had been almost purely the product of art—aping before the mirror. The ego's majestic "royal road" to ultimate silence, solitude (and supreme jouissance) must find its way being barred by the ethical, inept, monkey-king, who speaks the sacred truth of the egoist's fantasy—the fantasy we find intensified by postmodern consumer culture: to have an infinite capacity to need and to demand, to believe one can enjoy—but never to understand one's own desire.

This is why, perhaps, Lacan called for a return of desire (the other face of the Law). I think it is also why Freud was so attached to his art objects. For if we, like he, can see the horrifying face of an art pressed entirely into the service of a narcissistic collective (as with the Nazis or Reagan-era America), we can still not quite believe in the benignity of Fathers, nor await their return as fundamentalist religion (and possibly psychoanalysis?) does. We are stuck with art as the only Super-egoic form really available to us. If that is so, and I suspect Freud thought so too, a new stage of art and of science is here. Art must prize the artists who know that the mimetic image the mirror returns to them is less than ideal—rather an awkward Hanuman than Freud's Mikado-like figure[21] at the end of *Civilization and its Discontents,* rigidly adhering to the proscriptions of cultural order lest he lose his kingdom. And Science must remind him that his real "father" was a monkey—that his divinely ideal genealogy is no more than a "descent from the lower animals." Such are the much needed constraints on Narcissus required by the ego's era.

The alternative is murder in the rue Morgue. Poe's orangutan[22] is our simian brother, whose mastery of the mimicry of language (contra Descartes) authorizes the murder of not one but two women, and whose strictly amoral "art"—his ability to ape man—fulfills all the criteria of a "Kantian" aesthetic (perhaps he is Freud's daydreamer?) wherein art produces neither use nor meaning, but only narcissistic value.

4

The Freudian Things: Construction and the Archaeological Metaphor

Kenneth Reinhard

Freud's famous "archaeological metaphor" has frequently been invoked as an adequate and compelling figure for the logic and practice of psychoanalysis—a metaphor which, seemingly with Freud's authorization, has taken on the stature of a self-evident credo rather than a crucial yet ambiguous trope. Such appropriations of the metaphor figuratively stratify the psyche by portraying psychoanalysis as a process of plumbing the subject's unconscious "depths" and bringing repressed material to the conscious "surface." In this model, the work of psychoanalysis is understood as a therapeutic hermeneutics, a process of discovery in which the obscured past is revealed and integrated into the self-present ego. The archaeological metaphor thus has become the master trope which not only maps the "undiscovered country" of the psyche, but also reproduces its own binary structure in psychologistic models of the subject, the object, and their interpretation. Freud's rhetorical use of the metaphor, however, tends to complicate rather than confirm these assumptions, as well as the assumptions about the logic of metaphor which underlie them. In Freud's early work on hysteria, his later writings on obsessional neurosis, and his final essays on technique, the archaeological metaphor articulates the difficult relationship of truth and method in psychoanalysis, a relationship which the metaphor had served at once to enunciate and obscure. By following the implications of his theory and practice from its early hysterical formations to the paranoid limits of its logic in his late notion of "construction," Freud can no longer figure psycho-analysis as the "archaeological excavation" of a stratified psyche without confronting the traumatic, psychotic kernel which both occasions and distorts that metaphorics.

Freud's extensive collection of antiquities has often been re-garded as a kind of objective correlative for the archaeological met-aphor, the fragments of a phylogenic past which symbolize the retrieved secrets of individual ontogeny—including, for some com-mentators, that of Freud himself as "obsessive" collector. But while the presence of Freud's many Greek, Roman, Egyptian, and Jewish artifacts may appear to lend material support to the metaphor's to-pography of surface and depth, Freud's antiquities also bear silent witness to a Lacanian *topologics,* in which the object is cast not as the obscure object of analytic desire, but as its fundamentally lost "cause." For Lacan, Freud's antiquarian things are less metaphors of the psychoanalytic process or symptoms of his acquisitive per-sonality than they are manifestations of what Lacan calls the Freud-ian "Thing." Derived from Freudian and Heideggerian notions of *das Ding,* The Thing, for Lacan, is the traumatic materiality that both gives rise to and is sublimely in excess of the symbolic catego-ries of exchange, attribute, and positionality which determine the symbolic structure of the object. According to Lacan, Freud's antiq-uities are sublimated to the status of the Thing, the subject's orig-inary cause or *chose,* by their very situation as members of a collection. From this Lacanian point of view, the Freudian things can serve as the model for a psychoanalytic and critical practice of "construction," the Freudian technique, which, rather than mining the subject's unconscious for its treasure of hidden meanings, at-tempts to shift the subject's relationship to "meaning" as such. Criticizing the *"hermeneutic demand"* which "seeks" and thus in-variably finds a "never exhausted signification," Lacan constructs an epigraph for analytic practice by quoting Picasso: *"I do not seek, I find"* (S XI 7–8). "Finding" isolates the moment of chance en-counter, of stumbling onto or even over something, that distin-guishes psychoanalytic reading from traditional hermeneutics. It is in this sense that Freud's collection is a construction, a gathering of objects lost and found.

1. Hysterical Excavations: Symptom, Stigmata, *Sinthomata*

The archaeological metaphor first emerges in Freud's writings in his early essay "The Aetiology of Hysteria" (1896), returns in his case histories of Dora (1905 [1901]) and the Rat Man (1909), and makes its last major appearance in his late essay on technique, "Constructions in Analysis" (1937). For Freud's biographers, the figure is a key symbol for psychoanalysis, the "master metaphor for [Freud's] life's work" (Gay 172), a work defined by "a constant process of resuscitation, a bringing to light submerged memories and impulses of the past" (Jones III 318). Critics, whether affirming or challenging the value of the archaeological metaphor, tend to agree in their assumptions about its epistemological basis and ethical significance. Thus while Donald Spence criticizes Freud's metaphor, arguing that it implies a positivism to which the "so-called data" of psychoanalysis, "anecdotal rather than archival," are inadequate (79), Donald Kuspit responds to Spence by championing Freud's "mighty metaphor," insisting that in fact psychoanalysis achieves the positive interpretive goals of an "archaeological hermeneutics" (137) more fully than archaeology itself:

> Archaeologists must learn to live with it—learn to live with ignorance, learn like Tantalus to live with the object of their intellectual desire permanently out of reach—but psychoanalysts can sooner or later see their objects whole and clear, and hold them fast. Freud privileges psychoanalysis with true knowledge: this is when it leaves archaeology behind. (140)

For Kuspit, psychoanalysis transcends archaeology's fundamental limitations and even "ignorance" in its "true knowledge" of "whole and clear" objects, hidden meanings which the analyst, like the tragic hero, "has only to discover" (139).[1] In Kuspit's account of the empirical superiority of psychoanalysis, archaeology's failure to attain its object reaches mythological proportions in its ever "tantilized" desire. But Kuspit's reference to Tantalus seems curiously more applicable to psychoanalysis than archaeology, insofar as Tantalus' fate is not merely never to achieve the object of his desire, but

precisely never to learn to live without it—never to abandon his desire. Eternally but faithlessly striving to quench his thirst, Tantalus
is an apt figure of the psychoanalytic subject, cast in the shadow of
desire's infinite deferral of its evanescent object.[2]

Freud's earliest major use of the metaphor in "The Aetiology
of Hysteria" (1896) already suggests a certain epistemological
incommensurability between the projects of psychoanalysis and
archaeology:

> Imagine that an explorer arrives in a little-known region where
> his interest is aroused by an expanse of ruins, with remains of
> walls, fragments of columns, and tablets with half-effaced and un-
> readable inscriptions. He may content himself with inspecting
> what lies exposed to view, with questioning the inhabitants—per-
> haps semi-barbaric people—who live in the vicinity, about what
> tradition tells them of the history and meaning [*Geschichte und
> Bedeutung*] of these archaeological remains [*monumentalen
> Reste*], and with noting down what they tell him—and he may
> then proceed on his journey. But he may act differently. He
> may have brought picks, shovels and spades with him, and he may
> set the inhabitants to work with these implements. Together
> with them he may start upon the ruins, clear away the rubbish,
> and, beginning from the visible remains, uncover what is buried.
> If his work is crowned with success, the discoveries are self-
> explanatory: the ruined walls are part of the ramparts of a palace
> or a treasure-house; the fragments of columns can be filled out
> into a temple; the numerous inscriptions, which, by good luck,
> may be bilingual, reveal an alphabet and a language, and, when
> they have been deciphered and translated, yield undreamed-of in-
> formation about the events of the remote past, to commemorate
> which the monuments were built [*zu deren Gedächtnis jene Mon-
> umente erbaut worden sind*]. *Saxa loquuntur!* (SE 3:192; SA 6:54)

In Freud's metaphor—or, in this extended form, we might say his
allegory—the archaeologist/psychoanalyst is an explorer (*For-
scher*) who momentarily pauses in his wanderings when his interest is piqued by unreadable signs and ruins which seem to indicate
the presence of some obscure and ancient structure. Freud's primary purpose in the allegory is evidently to show that, rather than

subscribe to his patient's "superficial" account of the aetiology of
his neurotic symptoms (the local "semi-barbaric" inhabitants' version of the ruin's history and meaning), the analyst must work with
the analysand to "uncover what is buried" and rebuild the revealed
fragments into the true "history of the origin of the illness" (SE 192;
SA 54). But while a successful dig is defined in Freud's parable by
the discovery of a palace, treasure-house, or temple containing a
"self-explanatory" meaning, the analyst-as-archaeologist finds only
the scattered remnants (*Reste*) of edifices which must be "filled
out" and "translated" before they become meaningful. Moreover,
the monuments that are unearthed are not so much *of* the past as
to the past, built by lost civilizations to "commemorate" their own
passing. That is, the monument that was originally intended to im-
mortalize its historical moment in stone disintegrates into relics or
fossils which mutely record the inexorable passage of time. As
Freud's Latin motto ("*Saxa loguuntur*") suggests, if the relics of antiquity speak to the analytic reader, they always speak of something
other than the moment which they were intended to represent, and
always in the foreign and stony tongue of untimely epitaphs.

Freud continues by referring his allegory to Breuer's account
of hysterical symptoms:

> If we try, in an approximately similar way, to induce the symp-
> toms of a hysteria to make themselves heard as witnesses to the
> history of the origin of the illness, we must take our start from Jo-
> sef Breuer's momentous discovery: *the symptoms of hysteria*
> (apart from the stigmata) *are determined by certain experiences
> of the patient's which have operated in a traumatic fashion and
> which are being reproduced in his psychical life in the form of
> mnemic symbols* [Erinnerungssymbole]. (SE 3:192–3; SA 6:54–5)

According to Freud, the problem of analyzing hysterical symptoms
is "approximately similar" to that of interpreting archaeological
artefacts. But while both artefact and symptom may provide indications about the meaning (*Geschichte und Bedeutung*) of the past,
unlike the archaeologist, whose ruins, Freud writes, commemorate
history through and as "*Gedächtnis*," the hysteric's symptoms are

62 *Excavations and their Objects*

"mnemic symbols" [*Erinnerungssymbole*]. In Paul de Man's reading of Hegel's opposition between *Erinnerung* (remembrance) and *Gedächtnis* (memory), *Erinnerung* connotes "recollection as the inner gathering and preserving of experience" (1982: 771), the act of remembrance in which the past is interiorized and integrated in a symbolic system, while *Gedächtnis* implies rote memorization or mechanical recording of names, the "machinelike exteriority, the outward turn" towards arbitrary signs upon which thought depends (773).[3] The difference between the *Erinnerung* of hysterical symptoms and the *Gedächtnis* of archaeological artefacts is not deliberate in Freud's essay, but rather itself operates, we could say, at the level of *Gedächtnis*, reiterated in his writings with a drive-like insistence rather than systematized as a symbolic opposition. The epistemo-therapeutic imperative of American ego psychology can be expressed in these terms as the dialectical transformation of the machinic repetitions of unconscious *Gedächtnis* into the introjective rememoration of self-conscious *Erinnerung*. But far from negating the archaeological metaphor, such an understanding of the difference between the strange hieroglyphs of archaeological *Gedächtnis* and the familiar (and familial) symbols of psychoanalytic *Erinnerung* works in the service of its hermeneutical project, insofar as the distinction is posited only in order to be abolished.

Freud, however, parenthetically notes an exception to Breuer's rule of hysteria's process of symbolic reproduction, a recalcitrant non-signifying element in the conversion neuroses which interferes with the dialectical transformation of oblique symptom into revealed meaning: the "stigmata," the marginally somatic, non-ideogenic elements of hysterical symptomology which are uninterpretable, hence untreatable by psychoanalysis. Originally noted and named by Charcot, the stigmata are first characterized in Freud's writings as "highly obscure" and remain speculative knots throughout his early work on hysteria (SE 1: 148). In the co-authored *Studies on Hysteria* (1893–95), Josef Breuer describes the stigmata's strange interior-exterior position in relation to hysteria:

If the stigmata spring directly from this innate breeding-ground of hysteria and are not of ideogenic origin, it is also impossible to

give ideogenesis such a central position in hysteria as is sometimes done nowadays. What could be more genuinely hysterical
than the stigmata? They are pathognomonic findings which establish the diagnosis; and yet precisely they seem not to be ideogenic. But if the basis of hysteria is an idiosyncracy of the whole
nervous system, the complex of ideogenic, psychically deter-
mined symptoms is erected on it as a building is on its founda-
tions. And it is a building of *several storeys*. (SE 2: 244; Fischer
1970: 198)

The stigmata are the exceptions which prove the symbolic rule of
hysteria: the signal marks which confirm a diagnosis of hysteria,
the most "genuinely hysterical" of symptoms, yet themselves not
part of hysteria's field of representation, but exterior to the processes of symbolic conversion, emerging without mediation from
hysteria's "innate breeding ground" [*Mutterboden*]—literally, its
maternal ground.[4] While Breuer's foundation/house figure echoes
the stratification of Freud's archaeological metaphor, the notion of
the stigma indicates an uncanny surplus, both prior to and remaining after the psychoanalytic metaphor of surface and depth. The
stigma is the original "idiosyncracy," the hypothetical psychosomatic aberration on which the ideogenic symptoms of hysteria
are established, as well as part of "a very large residue [*Rest*] of un-
explained phenomena left over" from the theory of hysterical representation which it helps to found.

We can align the "stigmata" of early psychoanalysis with what
Lacan calls in his late seminars the *"sinthome"*—the non-analyzable
portion of the symptom which binds the three knotted orders of the
imaginary (meaning, consistency), the symbolic (lack, hole), and
the real (impossibility, ex-sistence). In the 1950s Lacan had defined
the symptom as a metaphor which symbolizes and condenses an unconscious signifier of sexual trauma.[5] The *sinthome,* according to
Lacan in the 70s, is the symptom in is function as a "stigma of
the real":a mote of significant *jouissance* which indicates or cites
the real, but has no rhetorical connection to it—signifies the real
precisely as that which forecloses all signification.[6] Slavoj Zizek
describes the *sinthome* as "a certain signifying formation pene-
trated with enjoyment: it is a signifier as a bearer of *jouis-sense,*

enjoyment-in-sense" (75). The *sinthome* is the insufferable enjoyment of the symptom that at once leads the hysteric to psychoanalysis, permeates the language of the analytic situation, and is left over
from symbolic interpretation, insofar as the hysteric refuses to give
up the symptom.

In as much as the "stigmata," like the *sinthome,* mark precisely those sedimentations within hysteria which resist hysterical
symbolization, remaining obscurely and intransigently material,
the opposition between the archaeology *Gedächtnis* of dead monuments and the psychoanalytical *Erinnerung* of living symbols and
symptoms arrives at a zero degree where such an opposition, rather
than abolished, becomes in-significant. Neither simply foreign to
hysteria nor fully within it, the stigmata are, in Lacan's expression,
"extimate"—intimately exterior—to both the theory and phenom-
enology of the symptom. Thus, if Freud's archaeological metaphor
is often appropriated by self-styled "depth" psychologies in the service of the hermeneutical re-production of the imaginary structure
of the ego, the metaphor may nevertheless precisely *as metaphor*
hit on something real. For while the symptom, according to Lacan,
is a metaphor, "it is not a metaphor to say so . . . For the symptom
is a metaphor whether one likes it or not" (*Écrits* E: 175).[7] That is,
it is not sufficient to imagine that the hysterical symptom is "like"
a metaphor insofar as, e.g., its displacement of the compromise between a desire and a prohibition may be analogized to the substitution and condensation of signifiers attributed to metaphor by Lacan
and Roman Jakobson. Rather, the symptom *is* a metaphor: a purely
linguistic process of supplementation enacted on the body, involv-
ing not only the symbolic and imaginary valences of the metaphorical production of meaning, but also the petrified *inconsistencies*
which emerge in metaphor's temporal extension into allegory—the
excessive or deficient materiality of signification which the metaphorical relationship between surface and depth screens and leaps
over.[8] Furthermore, we can understand the archaeological metaphor in this sense as itself a "symptom" of psychoanalysis: a metaphor of a metaphorical logic which nevertheless contains and
conceals a missed encounter produced by the deferred temporality
of allegory. The too-early or too-late of this "missing" within metaphor is the residuum left over from its movement of signification,

the precipitation of the gaps—the stigmata and *sinthomata*—of its own expressive structure.

2. Obsessive Theories: Preservation, Destruction, Eruption

In his case history of the Rat Man in "Notes Upon a Case of Obsessional Neurosis" (1909), Freud again has recourse to the archaeological metaphor, this time to explain the theory of psychoanalysis to his obsessive patient:

> I then made some short observations upon *the psychological differences between the conscious and the unconscious,* and upon the fact that everything conscious was subject to a process of wearing-away, while what was unconscious was relatively unchangeable; and I illustrated my remarks by pointing to the antiques standing about in my room. They were, in fact, I said, only objects found in a tomb, and their burial had been their preservation: the destruction of Pompeii was only beginning now that it had been dug up. (SE 10: 176; Fischer 1982: 25)

Here Freud expands the archaeological metaphor, directly supported by the material presence of his antiquities, into a three-part analogy in order to distinguish unconscious from conscious and to explain the therapeutic efficacy of interpretation. Just as funerary relics are preserved in a tomb, so Pompeii was buried under the lava and ash of Vesuvius, and so too the material of the conscious is concealed by the force of repression in the unconscious. Moreover, while their burial had been their preservation, both psychic and material objects once again become frangible by being brought to the light of day. The traditional Aristotelian symmetry of Freud's metaphor ("A is to B as C is to D"), however, is interrupted by the presence of the middle set of terms, Pompeii and Vesuvius, and the violent rhetorical twist Freud gives them. By reversing the expected associations of Vesuvius and archaeologist—casting the volcano's eruption as the "preservation" of Pompeii, and the archaeologist's excavation as its "destruction"—Freud's figure remains archaeological only by drastically rewriting the meaning of "archaeology," so that the analyst is now located in the strange position of the apocalyptic harrower of the unconscious, healing by fire and brim-stone. With this figural inversion, the artefacts on Freud's desk no longer stand for the trophies of recovered unconscious meanings, but the shattered fragments—or perhaps better, the shrunken heads—left over by the psychoanalytic "destruction" of the forces of repression.

The Rat Man, as Freud's account continues, is understandably perturbed by the image and skeptical about both the predictability and desirability of the methodology it implies:

> Was there any guarantee, he next enquired, of what one's attitude would be towards what was discovered? One man, he thought, would no doubt behave in such a way as to get the better of his self-reproach, but another would not.—No, I said, it followed from the nature of the circumstances that in every case the affect would be overcome—for the most part during the progress of the work itself. Every effort was made to preserve Pompeii, whereas people were anxious to be rid of tormenting ideas like his. (SE 10: 177)

In response to the Rat Man's concern that perhaps he would not want or be able to dislodge the "unknown content" (176) which analysis might finally discover, Freud retains the original structure of the analogy, but now distinguishes archaeological objects from psychological ideas [*Ideen*]. Unlike the valued relics of Pompeii, the contents of the unconscious are "tormenting" [*peinigende*]; thus, while the work of the archaeologist is now more conventionally presented as the preservation of Pompeii, the psychoanalyst re-mains the destroyer of the pathological affects of the unconscious. The middle terms of Pompeii-Vesuvius which had initially charged Freud's metaphor with paradox here return to undermine and even destroy it *as metaphor,* as a stable two-part system of analogies. In other words, if the *frisson* of the archaeological metaphor in this passage had at first been the reversal of the opposition between the meanings of "destruction" and "preservation," that opposition now dissolves altogether, as the metaphor's valence shifts indetermi-nately between the two.[9] The analyst now is more like a volcano than an archaeologist, but only insofar as the work of each is ambivalently to savage and to salvage. Freud's text, we could say, is it-self suspended without resolution between the preservation and the destruction of the archaeological metaphor, which itself becomes the unpredictable and threatening object of obsessive theorization. Just as the Rat Man feared, the work of analysis becomes ambiguous as its object is discovered to be ambivalent.

3. Psychosis: Construction and Interpretation

In his late essay "Constructions in Analysis" (1937), Freud once more compares psychoanalysis and archaeology, this time in the context of a discussion of the relationship of psychoanalytic in-terpretation and technique. The question of the consequences of what Freud calls "construction" for the truth-value of psychoanal-ysis had been an issue at least since the case of the Rat Man; Freud deals with it at length in the case of the Wolf Man (1918 [1914]), again in the "Case of Homosexuality in a Woman" (1920), and fi-nally here devotes an entire paper to the problem.[10] In "Construc-tions in Analysis," Freud discusses the veracity of analytic constructions as primarily a *clinical* and technical issue rather than an epistemological one: the truth at stake in the notion of construc-tion is not based on positivist assumptions about the difference be-tween fiction and reality, but on a psychoanalytic account of the material relationship between what Lacan calls the symbolic and the real. Ultimately, Freud's essay goes so far as to argue that the an-alyst's constructions have less in common with those of the archae-ologist than they do with the delusions of the psychotic—an uneasy kinship of method and madness which Freud had already suggested in the conclusion to his reading of Schreber's memoires.[11]

Freud begins by once more presenting the archaeological met-aphor in its "classical" form: the analyst's "work of construction, or, if it is preferred, of reconstruction, resembles to a great extent an archaeologist's excavation of some dwelling-place that has been de-stroyed and buried or of some ancient edifice" (SE 23: 259). Unlike the metaphor's tone of triumphant discovery in Freud's early work on hysteria, or its powerfully destructive connotations in his dis-

cussion of the Rat Man's obsessional neurosis, here analysis is cast
as archaeological in its *constructive* or reconstructive work. This
change reflects Freud's shifting theorization of psychoanalysis'
therapeutic motor from catharsis (1895), to interpretation (1900s),
to transference (1910s), and finally, in his last writings, to a notion
of technique inflected by his theorization of construction.[12] The
analogy here between archaeology and psychoanalysis is based on
the constructions or reconstructions each make, methods which
Freud at first does not distinguish and, moreover, claims are virtually "identical" in the two practices (259). The metaphor ultimately,
however, breaks down around the notion of construction, now dif-
ferentiated from "reconstruction": "But our comparison between
the two forms of work can go no further than this; for the main difference between them lies in the fact that for the archaeologist the
reconstruction is the aim and end of his endeavours while for
analysis the construction is only a preliminary labour" (260). Unlike archaeology's "aim and end" of reconstruction, psychoanalytic
construction is "preliminary" insofar as it must be followed by some
corroborative response from the analysand. It is "preliminary" not
in the sense of instigating a specific sequence of events, but rather
in its punctuation of the temporal unfolding of analysis: "the time
and manner in which [the analyst] conveys his constructions to
the person who is being analysed . . . constitute the link between
the two portions of the work of analysis" (SE 23: 259). Construction
is logically rather than chronologically preliminary to interpretation: a moment of disarticulating intervention, an invasive reorganization of the interpretive work of analysis with a narrative which
is almost by definition farfetched, egregiously extreme, a blatant
imposition—both merely and profoundly "constructed."

Thus, the difference between archaeology and psychoanalysis
replicates a certain heuristic distinction, according to Freud, between
"interpretation" and "construction" within psychoanalysis itself:

> If, in accounts of analytic technique, so little is said about 'con-
> structions' [*Konstruktionen*], that is because 'interpretations'
> [*Deutungen*] and their effects are spoken of instead. But I think

that 'construction' is by far the more appropriate description. 'Interpretation' applies to something that one does to some single element of the material, such as an association or a parapraxis. but it is a 'construction' when one lays before the subject of the analysis a piece [*Stück*] of his early history that he has forgotten. (SE 23: 261; SA 398)

Freud here discriminates between the local and ongoing work of interpretation, which traces the rhetorical movement of the analysand's language and actions, and the larger acts of intervention which characterize the analyst's constructions. While this opposition may appear to stage a dialectical progression from analysis to synthesis, in which all the "single elements" of interpretation are gathered together as a whole that explains the meaning of the analysand's life, we shall see that construction at once falls short of and exceeds the dialectical transumption it mimes.

In formulating a construction, the analyst is less concerned with its representational or historical accuracy than with its productivity within the analytic situation, indicated by the increase, decrease, or modification in the analysand's symptoms. Moreover, the manifestation of such change should not be taken as evidence of the construction's representational correspondence to either historical events or psychical fantasies. Rather than "true" or "false," we might, using J. L. Austin's terminology for performative utterances, call a construction which yields no effect whatsoever "infelicitous" and one that produces symptomatic reorganization, of whatever sort, "felicitous." As Freud writes, "indeed, we often get an impression as though, to borrow the words of Polonius, our bait of falsehood had taken a carp of truth" (262). The "truth" of the construction, that is, is not incompatible with its inaccuracy or even falseness as interpretive representation; the construction, in Polonius' expression, is the hook which can catch on truth (however fishy it may seem) while itself being no more than a lure. Freud's Shakespearean citation, moreover, suggests that his literary point of identification in this late essay has switched: if in *The Interpretation of Dreams* Freud identified with Hamlet as obsessional interpretive detective, here Freud has aligned himself with Polonius, the paranoid constructor of erotic fictions. Indeed, the reference indicates a larger turn in psychoanalytic attention from neurosis, as the exemplary object of analysis, to psychosis, as it estranged but specular other.

Concluding his essay with an extended comparison between psychoanalysis and psychosis, Freud again takes his figure of speech from Polonius: "The essence of it is that there is not only *method* in madness, as the poet has already perceived, but also a fragment of *historical truth* [*ein Stück* historischer Wahrheit]" (SE 23: 267; SA 405).[13] The narratives of both analytic construction and psychotic delusion contain what Freud calls a "fragment" or a "kernel" of truth. As Cynthia Chase suggests, Freud's essay implies that "the material of analysis's quest for 'historical truth' is delusions: constructs around the opaque, non-discursive contents (like the Wolf Man's word-things) of disavowals" (121). Rather than part of the symbolically-distorted narratives of history and neurosis, the fragment of truth common to the psychotic's delusion and the analyst's construction stems from what Freud calls a "terrible event" [*etwas Schreckliches*]—an originary trauma, in which something disavowed [*verleugnet*] is nevertheless preserved as a denied fragment of the real. Freud writes,

> The delusions of patients appear to me to be the equivalents of the constructions which we build up in the course of an analytic treatment—attempts at explanation and cure, though it is true that these, under the conditions of a psychosis [*den Bedingungen der Psychose*], can do no more than replace the fragment of reality [*das Stück Realität*] that is disavowed [*verleugnet*] in the present by another fragment that had already been disavowed in the remote past. It will be the task of each individual investigation to reveal the intimate connections between the material of the present disavowal [*gegenwärtigen Verleugnung*] and that of the original repression [*damaligen Verdrängung*]. Just as our construction is only effective because it recovers a fragment of lost experience, so the delusion owes its convincing power to the element of historical truth which it inserts in the place of the rejected reality. (SE 23: 268; SA 405)

Within the paranoid theories and narratives constructed by both
the psychotic and the psychoanalyst is a "piece" [*Stück*] of terrify-
ing and traumatic "historical truth." This is the residue of the in-
cursion of pain or hunger which in Freud's earlier linked essay,
"Negation" (1925)—textual fragments of which are literally incor-
porated into the essay on constructions—he had called *das Ding:*
the pre-subject's originary "extimacy," which, like the "stigmata" of
hysteria, persists as its condition of being. Near the end of "Construction in Analysis" Freud connects this thingly "fragment of lost
experience" with the complexity of the *Krankheitsverursachung,*
"the causation of the illness" (SE 23: 268); embedded in this com-
pound we find the German word for *cause,* "Ursache," which itself
breaks down into "ur" and "sache"—that is, into "primal" and "object." The core of the paranoid's delusion is thus "intimately" connected with the subject's "original" gesture of the repression or
foreclosure of a signifier which, in being refused from the symbolic
order, returns as the cause or *la chose* of the subject as well as of
the subject's delusion.[14] In Freud's "psychotic" construction of construction, the analyst precipitates a symptomatic response by invoking, whether intentionally or not, such a disavowed thingly
signifier which, although circulating with pathological consequences in fantasy, remains unintegrated into the subject's unconscious chain of signifiers. As the residue of a "terrible event," the
real Thing conjured by construction hangs between analyst and
analysand, the kernel of a *délire à deux* in excess of the dialectic of
negation and affirmation which sets the tempo for interpretation's
pas de deux.

Thus, the Freudian notion of "construction" ungrounds the
neurotic epistemology of the archaelogical metaphorics on which
it is based. Construction's affiliation with the real of psychotic delusion prevents its reduction to a hermeneutics for the production
of meaning or a therapeutics for the regulation of the ego. As such,
construction divides the practical ethics of psychoanalysis between
contradictory but equally necessary modes of reading. On the one
hand, psychoanalysis requires symbolic *interpretation:* the production of meaning through the movement from signifier to signifier,
from "manifest" to "latent," which both posits the conceptual

spaces of surface and depth for and of the subject, and invites their hermeneutical navigation. On the other hand, psychoanalysis entails *construction:* the realignment of the signifiers of interpretation into a contrived, virtually delusory, act of *citation* more than narration, an intervention which mobilizes and reconfigures the fixed points of fantasy.[15] By itself, interpretation would be no more than the prosthetic extension of the ego's self-productive narratives of resistance and defense. By itself, construction would be only "wild," or rather "crazy," analysis—that is, nothing more nor less than psychosis.

Construction thus is the confection of an assemblage of signifiers which is both greater and less than the sum of its parts. As Gerard Pommier writes, "the time of construction . . . has two consequences. On the one hand, the subject recognize himself there, and on the other, recognizing himself, he breaks through [*franchit*] the plane of imaginary identification where up to that point he had been immured" (157). Construction involves a moment of "recognition" which projects the subject in a fantasmatic image of unification, much like the dialectic of specular identification Lacan calls the "mirror stage." By hitting upon a traumatic "piece of early history" which the subject has internally excluded, however, construction also *breaks through* its own imaginary fabrications, and insists on the stigmata-like nodes in fantasy which refuse dialectical synthesis and hermeneutical signification. Construction, we could say, is the *supplement* of interpretation, an excess which both completes interpretation and leaves it in ruins. By constructing and confronting the traumatic signifier-thing left over from the fantasy of interpretation, psychoanalytic reading must walk a narrow path between merely imaginary identification and purely paranoid delusion.[16]

Thus Freud writes that the work of psychoanalysis "would consist in liberating the fragment of historical truth from its distortions and its attachments [*Entstellungen und Anlehnungen*] to the actual present day and in leading it back [*zurechtzurücken*] to the point in the past to which it belongs" (SE 23: 268; SA 405). Psychoanalytic construction is presented in this formulation as a *reverse archaeology:* neither the preservation nor destruction of the past, but an act which "frees" [*befreien*] the fragment of the real from its encasing figurations and disfigurations in order to *return it to the past*—not, however, through *Erinnerung,* redemptively integrated into consciousness as the rememoration of self, but by *Gedächtnis,* restored to the subject as both the most familiar and the most foreign thing, as, in Lacan's phrase, the non-signifying Thing "in you more than you" (S XI 263).

For Walter Benjamin, such a possibility of construction emerges for materialist criticism through the agency of the collector. In his late essay, "Eduard Fuchs, Collector and Historian," written in the same year as Freud's "Constructions in Analysis" (1937), Benjamin suggests that the dialectic of "collector" and "historian" embodied by Fuchs defines the ground of a historical materialism based on what Benjamin calls *construction:*

> Historicism presents an eternal image of the past, historical materialism a specific and unique engagement with it. The substitution of the act of construction for the epic dimension proves to be the condition [*Bedingung*] of this engagement. . . . The task of historical materialism is to set to work an engagement with history original [*ursprünglich*] to every new present. It has recourse to a consciousness of the present that shatters the continuum of history. [...] It is the dialectical construction which distinguishes that which is our original [*ursprünglich*] concern with historical engagement from the patchwork findings of actuality. (OWS: 352, fn. 4; GS II.2.468)

In order to "shatter" the timeless epic images and epochal continuities which historicism fashions into its narratives of the "actual," historical materialism must establish a "specific and unique" engagement with the past in the present—an engagement effected by and as an "act of construction." Benjamin correlates this project of a materialist "construction" of history with his early concept of *Ursprung* ("origin" or better, "primal leap") from his book on the Baroque theatre of mourning, *Ursprung des deutschen Trauerspiels.* Construction, for Benjamin, is the critic's assembly of the fragmentary ruins of the past into what Benjamin calls a "constellation," a collection which never fully totalizes, systematizes, or aestheticizes its members.[17] Historical materialism's construction is the work of *collection* which encounters and engages the *Ursprung* of objects, their transitory appearance and disappearance in each present moment, unlike historicism's examination of the merely "factual" content of history. Thus, as much as the "condition" [*Be-ding-ung*] of the dialectic of the collector and the historian, construction is the act *left over* by historical theorization. For Benjamin, himself a great collector of toys, books, and textual fragments, we could say that writing is an act of re-collection: not, however, a rememoration through the synthetic and historicist metaphors of *Erinnerung*, but only by and as the fragmentary allegorical consciousness of *Gedächtnis*. Re-collection, that is, re-constellates an array of ancient and modern relics into a construction whose *Ursprung*, its origination and passing, marks both the condition and the limitation of any materialist textual history.

4. Lacan: The Freudian Things

In Lacan's seminars and writings, the analyst is portrayed not as a Heinrich Schliemann who triumphantly uncovers the meaning of the classical past and the "classical" complexes, but as an Orpheus who descends to hell rather than Troy, always returning empty-handed. In *Seminar XI* Lacan writes, "we have, in Eurydice twice lost, the most potent image we can find of the relation between Orpheus the analyst and the unconscious" (25). Lacan represents psychoanalysis less as the discovery of the lost secrets of the unconscious than as the endless re-discovery of the unconscious *as lost:* as a primary rupture, a traumatic encounter, a missed appointment. Psychoanalysis, according to Lacan, must work against the ego's imperialism and counter its illusions of mastery, wholeness, and monolithic meaning. Thus Lacan's emblems for the psychoanalyst are not Homeric or Virgilian heroes who remember the past, but Ovidian figures such as Orpheus, Tiresias, and Actaeon whom the past dis-members.[18]

The difference between the Orphic archaeology of Lacan and the Trojan historicism of Anglo-American ego psychology is evident in their nearly antithetical readings of the famous Freudian dictum, "*Wo Es war, soll Ich werden.*" For the editors of the Standard Edition, the line translates into: "where id was, there ego shall be" (SE 22: 80). This translation implicitly casts psychoanalysis as the ego's collaborator: working together, their manifest destiny and moral duty is to colonize the id and expand the empire of consciousness into the "undiscovered country" of the unconscious. For Lacan, however, the ego is not the subject's salvation, but merely its symptom: the ego is the projection of a defensive screen against the exigencies of both internal and external pain, an illusion of self-identity which analysis must dislodge, not reinforce. Thus in his early essay, "The Freudian Thing," Lacan polemically translates Freud's phrase as "There where it was . . . it is my duty that I should come to being" (Écrits E: 129). Lacan's translation reverses the vector of the psychoanalytic imperative, implying that the subject's ethical duty is to come to be in and *as* the unconscious—a radically ex-centric position, however, which offers no place for a unified self to stand. For Lacan, the *Wo Es war* insists that the subject take on "its" past as the foreign and unknowable language of someone else, the desire of the Other. The past-tense of the phrase, moreover, expresses this subjective ethics as the call of temporality: not, however, the historicist invitation to reclaim and transform the past, but as the injunction to assume the past *as passed*—that is, the call to be reclaimed *by* the signifiers of history. By the 1960s, Lacan reinflects the direction of this imperative to include the real; in *Seminar XI* he comments, "The subject is there to rediscover *where it was* . . . the real" (45). The "it" of the *Wo Es war* here indicates not only the unconscious as the symbolic order, but also as inhabited by the signifier in its materiality, the thingly residue of signification. In his 1965 essay "Science and Truth" Lacan glosses the ethics of the *Wo Es war* as "the paradox of an imperative that presses me to assume my own causality" (13)—the necessity, that is, to assume the trauma of the past not as an external catastrophe that forced itself upon me, but as the material *cause* most foreign insofar as it is most intimately my own. The subject that emerges there is both *subjected to* (alienated into) and *subjectivized by* (separated from) the signifiers and desire of the Other. The ethical imperative of

Lacanian psychoanalysis, thus, takes up the call of a *reverse archae-ology:* the subject must attenuate its claims to unified meaning and unalienated being as an ego in order to punctually emerge and dis-appear "there," on the other side of its imaginary self-representations, in the gap in the symbolic order where the real irrupts.[19]

In *Seminar VII: The Ethics of Psychoanalysis,* Lacan's discus-sion of the difference between object and Thing leads him to com-ment on Freud's archaeological artefacts, by way of introduction to a "little apologue" on the nature of collecting:

> There is a lot to say on the psychology of the collection. I myself am a bit of a collector, and if some of you believe that it is in im-itation of Freud, you are welcome to think so. I believe that it is for entirely different reasons than his. I have seen the remains [*débris*] of Freud's collection on Anna Freud's shelves, and they seemed to me to highlight more of the fascination they exerted on him at the level of the signifier . . . than a well-informed taste for what is called an object. (135)

As a notorious bibliophile himself, Lacan accepts the obvious asso-ciation of his collecting habit with Freud's, while insisting on some unspecified but essential difference between their motives. At least a part of Lacan's objection here is to the suggestion that his collect-ing is in "imitation" of Freud—based, that is, on an *imaginary* iden-tification with him. For Lacan goes on to criticize such a specular construal of Freud's relationship to his collection: rather than a group of imaginary objects that would support the collector's sense of self by reflecting his good "taste," the remnants left from Freud's collection, Lacan argues, are evidence of a certain "fascination" which operates at the level of the "signifier." That is, while Freud's collection articulates a symbolic series whose meaning is deter-mined by metonymic contiguity and metaphoric substitution, the *fascination* of the objects, although emerging from this figurative distribution, is a function of their sublimation beyond their sym-bolic value, into the position of the Thing.[20]

From the vantage of his later work, *Seminar VII* will be seen as marking the beginning of Lacan's reinflection of the psychoanalytic object from its primary association with the imaginary to its increasing affiliation with the real. Such retrospection allows us to read the "fascination" Lacan ascribes to Freud's artefacts not as an imaginary characteristic, but as implicating them in the brilliant, glittering thing-ness which Lacan will attribute to the *objet a* in his next year's seminar on transference.[21] The real-ity of the *objet a*, the theoretical intersection of object and Thing, lies not in some supposed "deep" noumenal essence beyond its phenomenal manifestation, but precisely in its emergence as *pure semblance* in a gap in the symbolic order. Thus, the non-specular "fascination" of Freud's antiquities is a function of neither what they look like (their imaginary similitudes) nor what they represent (their symbolic interpretations), but their constitution as signifier-things in a collection. Like signifiers, that is, they promise a legibility which they deny; like things, they opaquely, mutely point only to themselves.

Lacan explains this sublime effect of Freud's artefacts *qua* objects in a collection through an account of his friend Jacques Prévert's collection of match boxes. The "extremely agreeable" effect of the group of match boxes, uninteresting in themselves, was a result of their arrangement in an interlocking chain running up and down the walls of a room:

> I believe that the effect of shock or novelty produced by this collection of empty match boxes—this point is essential—was to bring out something we perhaps dwell on too little: a box of matches is not simply an object, but can rather, in the guise or *Erscheinung* in which it was offered up in a truly imposing multiplicity, be a Thing . . . . The completely gratuitous, proliferating and superfluous, almost absurd character of this collection, in fact gets at the box of matches' thingness [*choséité*]. Thus the collector finds his motive in this mode of apprehension which bears less on the box of matches than on this Thing which subsists in a box of matches. (S VII: 136)

While the sublimation of the match boxes is not identical with the sublime effect of their seemingly endless metonymic extension within an infinitely expanding symbolic order, it nevertheless is a function of that proliferation. Each box, Lacan tells us, is connected to the next by having its drawer pushed into the back of the one in front of it; each, therefore, is *filled by a void* created by its penetration by the empty drawer of its neighbor. The thingness of each box is a function of its constitutive yet foreign hollowness, since it is only in the boxes' arrangement as an interpenetrating *collection* that "thingness" emerges as such for any individual box. The real Thing, we could say, "collects" in the interstices left by the interminable movement of the chain of signifiers.[22] Freud's collection, like Prévert's, is also a constellation or assemblage of signifiers that, in the very superficiality of its appearance—its "completely gratuitous, proliferating and superfluous, almost absurd character"— exceeds its symbolic organization. Like a psychoanalytic construction, a collection is more than the sum of its parts; this "more than," however, designates not the harmonious synthesis of the beautiful—the ego's last defense against the real—but the numerical excesses of the sublime.[23]

In his essay "Unpacking My Library: A Talk About Book Collecting" (1931), Benjamin describes the collector's relationship to things as "a relationship to objects [*Dingen*] which does not emphasize their functional, utilitarian value . . . but studies and loves them as the scene, the stage, of their fate [*Schicksals*]" (60; GS IV.1. 389). The "fate" for which the collector loves the collected objects is not merely the accidents of their historical or material provenance, but rather the determination of the collector by the things whose possession itself possesses him:

> For a collector—and I mean a real collector, a collector as he ought to be—ownership is the most intimate relationship that one can have to objects [*Dingen*]. Not that they come alive in him; it is he who lives in them. So I have erected one of his dwellings, with books as the building stones, before you, and now he is going to disappear inside, as is only fitting. (67; 396)

According to Benjamin, it is not the inevitable dispersal of the collection, but the disappearance of the *collector* that is at issue in the temporal relationship to the collected things. Collecting for Benjamin, and *writing as collecting,* we could say, enacts a critical version of the *Wo Es war,* a practice of reverse archaeology, an ethics of coming to be in the real of the Thing. Perhaps too, it is only fitting, that Freud, whose cremated ashes finally came to rest in one of the ancient urns of his own collection, should come so literally to dwell in the hollow center of the Thing.

5

Father Figures in Freud's Autoaesthetics

Stephen Barker

That Freud made a quite impressive collection of objects of various kinds from antiquity is itself most interesting, from the points of view of memory, as a link to the past, aesthetics, as a sign of the *Kunsttrieb*,[1] and economics: even when he could barely afford the luxury of so doing he continued to add to his ever-growing accumulation. His fascination not just with the cultures from which the objects came, but with the evidence of the art-drive, the very remnants, traces, and reminders of those cultures—those collectible objects themselves, all of which shared a personal (or, as Lacan points out, an intimately exterior) relationship with Freud—adds a provocative dimension to this innovative thinker whose ties with the past were more prominent than with the future he so significantly influenced. The relationship of past and future itself fascinated Freud, who concluded *The Interpretation of Dreams* with the following assertion:

> And what of the value of dreams in regard to our knowledge of the future? That, of course, is out of the question. One would like to substitute the words: 'in regard to our knowledge of the past.' For in every sense a dream has its origin in the past. . . . By representing a wish as fulfilled the dream certainly leads us into the future; but this future, which the dreamer accepts as his present, has been shaped in the likeness of the past by the indestructible wish. (471)

One is indeed tempted to see Freud's collection of antiquities as objectified wishes, "representations" of a departed but valued past that are, if not indestructible, at least physical and enduring. A work of art, for Freud, as manifestation of the art-drive, is always the fulfillment of a wish, a rarified focus for meaning, significance, value; in its objective transformation of recalcitrant materials, it is the alchemical marriage of the pleasure principle (as wish) and the reality principle, in the form of a symbolic object.[2] Further, according to Freud, works of art insist on speculative response from the viewer/collector (which amounts to a complex structuration of imagination, articulation, and interpretation, in process necessitating a re-fabrication of the object and the "subject" responding) defining their symbolic power.

Freud's method of display of his antiquities in his study leads to further speculation regarding their symbolic power. Many pieces rest in glass-fronted display cases resembling caskets, from which at the same time Freud could glimpse them and *they* could be imagined to look out at Freud's study; others are arranged like a Greek chorus around the room on shelves, mantel, walls; still others appear like friends, colleagues, or some diminutive community of elders at the edge of the writing pad on his desk. In any case, Freud's collection, as well as the way he displayed it first in Vienna and then in London, compels us to speculate on its power in Freud's psychic and aesthetic life and in the greater arena of his aesthetic theory, since clearly Freud attached great weight not only to the possession of these objects but to their arrangement in the microcosm of his study as well.

Freud himself, of course, would vehemently discourage us from such speculation: as a sign of his commitment to the science of psychology, he took a famously dismissive view of speculative thought, as opposed to "solid" investigation. But spying a subliminal strategy in Freud's anti-speculation, I want here, in what follows, to speculate on Freud's collected figures, their deep relation to his general aesthetic, the historical figuration on which that aesthetic is founded, and the *selbtdarstellung* (as "self-fashioning") Freud's collection of antiquities signifies. Freud's trepidation concerning abstract speculation is well-founded, of course: speculation is always dangerous, what Derrida in *The Post Card*'s "To Specu-late—On Freud" calls "asking questions in the dark, or in a penum-bra, rather, the penumbra in which we keep ourselves when Freud's unanalyzed reaches out its phosphorescent antennae" (278). Der-rida's complex Platonic metaphor, bracketing that enigmatic "Freud's unanalyzed" which so magically reaches toward the pur-gatorial abysses of speculation, identifies the philosopher in Freud, an echo of Nietzsche who, from the penumbra, speculates appar-ently without need of the verification the scientific methodology whose distant "absolute light" Freud requires.

But one must not rush too quickly to judge Freud's anti-speculation at face value. Freud as always is elusive and finally quite enigmatic concerning speculation as the ground of philosophy: "as a young man," he wrote to Fliess (4 February 1896, just months be-fore he began to collect his antiquities), "I know no longing other than for philosophical knowledge, and now I am about to fulfill it as I move from medicine to psychology." Freud's "metapsychology" (his word) relies on speculative assumptions similar to and drawn directly from speculative philosophy, and which pays back to that philosophy a rich treasure of aesthetic concerns.[3] Indeed, since one of my chief purposes is to juxtapose Freud and Nietzsche, it must be noted that Freud is if anything *more* philosophical than Nietzsche, who wanted to replace philosophy with his metaphysical *Wille zur Macht* as a completion of the fictionalization of self-discovery. Both Nietzsche and Freud, from their differing viewpoints, might have adapted Abraham Kaplan's introductory statement in "Freud and Modern Philosophy," "philosophy is culture become self-conscious" (209), Freud changing "philosophy" to "psychology," Nietzsche chang-ing not a word.

But speculations on Freud can ground itself on good evidence: the very artifacts Freud collected. And one is invited in approaching Freud's artworks to consider the metaphoric conversions of specu-lation and (self-) interpretation, and to come to terms with Freud's history of repressions, forgettings, and repudiations, the most sa-lient of which in terms of his collection being repudiations of spec-ulation, of Nietzsche, and of his traditional (paternal) culture. These seeming repudiations are all in fact aesthetic sublimations;

the figures Freud collected—after his father Jakob's death—are
sublimated father figures exercising complex relationships with the
five manifestations of the Freudian father (among many others) on
whom I want to concentrate here in the context of Freud's strategic,
autoaesthetic self-fabrication.[4]

Ironically, given Freud's concern with memory and the narrative of memory, one of the central strategies of such self-formulating
speculation, and of art collecting in general, is selectivity, whose
thematic form is *leaving out,* abbreviating, forgetting. Forgetting
(*vergesse*) is an enabling procedure, since to remember fully is to
remember super-abundantly and thus to be incapacitated. Forgetting, as selectivity and as narrative construction, is central to Freud,
with regard to objects from the past. Freud's collection stands as a
diverse monument not only to remembered cultures of the past, but
to their *loss,* to our inability to remember them. Indeed, the past is
in some very real ways repressed, re-constructed, or misrepresented
in Freud's artifacts, particularly in their use-value to him. This connection between forgetting and repression is forged clearly and in
remarkably Freudian terms by Nietzsche, who asserts that

> forgetting is no mere *vis inertiae* as the superficial imagine; it is
> rather an active and in the strictest sense positive faculty of re-
> pression, that is responsible for the fact that what we experience
> and absorb enters our consciousness as little while we are digest-
> ing it (one might call the process 'inpsychation') as does the thou-
> sandfold process, involved in psychical nourishment—so-called
> 'incorporation.' (*On the Genealogy of Morals* I.1)

The dangers and the excitement of forgetting give rise to excavation, whose (forgetful) object in Freud is to reach the fully achiev-
able "truth" buried within, however much this simplistic notion
may have been undermined in Post-Freudian thought. His ancient
objects serve as incorporations of and at the same time surrogates
for that truth, as well as remembrances of its invention forgetting
itself in the guise of re-discovery. In terms of the larger aesthetic issues represented by and in his collection, Freud wants us to interpret art as he does dreams: in art we can claim to discover the
archaic beneath what seems to be new, and of the new concealed
within that which seems most archaic; interpretation of art "makes

possible the understanding of themes borrowed from individual or collective memory," in Sarah Kofman's words. Thus, as Kofman points out, between the psychoanalyst and the archaeologist,

> the psychologist has the advantage. In archaeology, important fragments are lost forever and cannot be joined to the pieces at hand, which means that archaeological reconstructions are merely plausible. But the psychic object whose prehistory is to be reconstructed is different; . . . it may be doubted whether any psychical structure can really be the victim of total destruction. (69)

Art objects such as those Freud collected carry within them, according to his tendentious concept of them, a wholeness and solidity, as well as a stimulating or inspiring power, he tells us we cannot doubt nor deny.

And yet forgetting, which enables the archaeologist and the analyst, is also a source of suffering, to the eradication of which Freud dedicated his professional life. One ends suffering by canceling threat—chiefly the threat of the Other, whether society, the father, or internal or external sources of power over which one has no control, to which one might become subordinated, and which might produce debilitating fear. Art, for Freud (making it, owning it, appreciating it, interpreting it, collecting it), like psychoanalysis, exists in some global way to relieve suffering. This relief requires various kinds of forgetting of suffering and, in terms of Freud's strategic self-enabling, here is one of the great differences between Freud and Nietzsche. While Freud's aim is "to transform neurotic despair into the general unhappiness which is the usual lot of mankind" (Kaplan 229), Nietzsche's metapsychology embraces suffering. So for Freud Nietzsche too must be strategically forgotten. Here we have a first glimpse, within the realm of speculative thought, of the fact that Freud's aesthetic consists of a series not of excavations but of layered re-interments, of which Nietzsche's thought is only one. A vital key to this dialectic of concealment and revelation is to be found in the extraordinary statement with which Ernest Jones begins Volume Two of his *Life and Work of Sigmund Freud:*

> In 1901 Freud, at the age of forty-five, had attained complete maturity, a cnsummation of development that few people really

Illustration 1.   Sigmund Freud and his father, Jakob, eight and forty-eight years old.

achieve. . . . A profound self-confidence had been masked by strange feelings of inferiority, even in the intellectual sphere, and he had tried to cope with these by projecting his innate sense of capacity and superiority on to a series of mentors on some of whom he then became curiously dependent for reassurance. (3)

Are we to take Jones seriously in this ingenuous and categorical description of Freud's so-called maturity? Are we to assume that the second part of the passage somehow follows on from the first, though they seem to be contradictory? And what are we to make of this set of statements as a biographical indicator of Freud's development (and its problematic relationship to his science)? How is this development possible, when that "profound self-confidence" by which Jones characterizes Freud all too quickly becomes another series of "dependencies." And even more importantly for Freud and the authority figures on whom he built his theories and against whom he reacted, who are these mentors on whom Freud "projects" himself for "reassurance"? For Jones, they are Brücke, Meynert, Fleichl, Charcot, Breuer, Fliess—professional colleagues in and around Freud's specific discipline. If we develop this theme of dependency, however, we discover that Freud's dependencies, as we might have suspected, extend far beyond the professional associations to which Jones makes reference. In fact, Freud spent his life in a complex series of dialogues with a constellation of "father figures" whose presence in his life reveals much not only about his framework as a psychoanalyst and psychological theorist, but about his aesthetic interests, and therefore his interests and tastes as a collector of art and antiquities, as well. Each of these father figures contributes something to the themes of 1) suffering, 2) forgetting, and 3) concealment and revelation that excavation, like psychoanalysis, suggests; it makes no difference whether these figures were real, corporeal beings or not, since each one, in terms of Freud's (auto)aesthetic, is a spirit, a *geist*, a complex function of Freud's worldview.

The first and most obvious father figure we must scrutinize, a figure preliminary to but underlying the present excavation, is

Illustration 2.   Jakob Freud at about 80.

Jakob Freud. A great deal has been written on the Freuds *père* and *fils*, and indeed Sigmund Freud's relationship with his father is most worthy of the separate treatment it has received, but it is not the Jakob Freud of Sigmund's early life that is of interest here, but the already-dead Jakob, the "father *figure*" of the *dead* father. Sigmund Freud investigated and ruminated over the death and the fact of death of his father so extensively in his writings that it becomes quite striking. Though Freud's dead father is in fact chronologically the last father figure examined here, in terms of Freud's collecting the catalytic power of Jakob's death and wraith is a vitally important first. Following a troubled relationship with his son, Jakob Freud's death on 23 October, 1896, coincided with several occurrences in the life of Sigmund, then aged forty. On the night of Jakob's funeral, Freud *fils* had what he called a "pretty dream" in which he allowed himself to be late to Jakob's funeral, having been detained at the barbershop having his hair trimmed. A sign on the shop wall said "You are requested to close the eyes." The dream disturbed Freud and preoccupied him. The usual interpretation is that the dream accounts for Freud's guilt with regard to his Jewish father. Late to the funeral because of ego-centered vanity, Freud *fils* sits in the barber shop looking at a sign instructing him to take an obedient (blind) stance, and to close off the organs of aesthetic interpretation, the eyes.

Freud *fils* returned to the dream several times in his writings, and found in it two related meanings for him: "one should do one's duty towards the dead," an apology for not having done his duty to the dead father and a seeking of forgiveness for that oversight, and at the same time "one's duty" being the proper remembrance of the dead, keeping the dead one spiritually alive. The dream was thus "an outlet for the feeling of self-reproach which a death generally leaves among the survivors," acknowledging his divergence from the father's path into his own.

But these may be sublimated interpretations themselves. A careful reading of the dream gives rise to another interpretation, less simple but related, in which the dream acknowledges guilt but also the son's avoidance and sublimation of the father into an aesthetic of life emptied of the father. Thus, in the dream Freud is in the barbershop of his mundane life in Vienna, having his (egocentric/Mosaic) beard trimmed, instructed *not to see* what he is supposed to see, both in order to remake himself by taking power over oneself, and to fabricate his own path. Freud's late arrival at the funeral indicates his late arrival in a culture theretofore much more interesting, provocative, and substantial. In this reading, Jakob's death is a release, in two ways: first, Sigmund no longer eclipsed by the living father, and second, the sublimation of the father into a life-aesthetic in which Sigmund gathers signs of that buried past around himself. Genealogy sublimated into excavation, to allow the past to live again and to make it eternally corporeal in the memoria he gathered around him.

Much good evidence exists for this release hypothesis and for its effects. Sigmund wrote to Fliess on 2 November, 1896, a fortnight after the death of Jakob Freud, "by one of the obscure routes behind the official consciousness, the old man's death affected me deeply. . . . By the time he died his life had long been over, but at a death the whole past stirs within one" (Krüll 41). The "one" within whom the "whole past stirs" is of course Sigmund himself, who within months, by May of 1897, had begun the study that would eventuate in *On the Interpretation of Dreams* several years later. The idea of the stirring past, seen in the subconscious and in dreams (like the shades of Hades to Odysseus), offers Freud a direction for investigation and a new set of alienating and enabling conditions. The past cannot be brought back, and yet it must not be forfeited; the authority of the past must be reconciled with the burgeoning autonomy Freud felt in now "being his own man," nearing that full maturity of which Jones speaks so enigmatically.

The father's death catalyzed another response as well. At precisely this time and closely related to Jakob's death, Freud wrote to Fliess (6 December, 1896) that "I have now adorned my room with plaster casts of the Florentine statues. It was the source of extraordinary refreshment to me." And so begins Freud's collecting. The odd change in number here, from the plural of statues to the singular of the refreshment Freud felt, acknowledges that statues do not provide refreshment, but rather the acts of adornment by which they are added to his environment; not the objects themselves, but the sublimations they represent. Freud has begun, the letter indicates, to gather around him the icons of a physically dead but aesthetically living past, a past that resides within him, metaphorically, and that makes *him* feel not dead but alive again ("refreshed"). The threat of death is overcome in the metaphoric life of the past embodied in the figures with which he begins literally to surround himself and which, in them, can never be lost: they, and his ability to collect and instill restorative power in them, are a defense against death's disruption and an assertion of autoaesthetic power. The first father figure, the catalyst of Freud's growing self-hood, is the metaphoric preservation of the dead Jakob through his metaphoric proto-sublimation in Freud's recuperative statuary.[5] This symbolic proto-sublimation ("proto-" because Freudian sublimation, although it had already been identified by Nietzsche, had not yet been defined by Freud) had been in evidence from early in Sigmund's life, but quite literally burst forth, following the catalyst of Jakob's death, into the ever-growing iconic forest surrounding Freud in his study.

One of Jakob Freud's most vehement instructions to his son had been to avoid investigating the past, to re-fashion the future out of the present. Following Jakob's death, Freud had a year-long crisis in which he had to deal with the taboo against investigating the past that Jakob had placed on him. The death of the father freed him to investigate not only the past but the taboo itself. According to Fliess, Freud again made use of the archaeological metaphor to do so:

> I am working on the assumption that our psychical mechanism has come about by a process of stratification: the material present in the shape of memory-traces is from time to time subjected to a rearrangement in accordance with fresh circumstances—is, as it were, transcribed. Thus what is essentially new in my theory is the thesis that memory is present not once but several times over, that it is registered in various species of 'signs.' (Krüll 43)

"Repression" is thus an "imperfect system of signs," an "inadequate translation" of the past. Indeed, repression becomes for Freud "a failure of translation," a "pathological defense" against "memory traces from an earlier phase which have not yet been translated"

(Krüll 43).[6] Without doubt, Freud's psychical excavations came about as a result of the crisis fomented by the father's death in 1896, which resulted in the repudiation of the 1893 seduction theory and the discovery of the phantasy life of the young psyche in which wish-fulfillment, the fictions of the drive-oriented mind, is more powerful than any exterior reality. This study, catalyzed by Jakob's death, led directly to *The Interpretation of Dreams,* though Freud himself did not make the direct connection until 1908, when he wrote the second preface to the work:

> For this book had a further subjective significance for me person-
> ally—a significance which I only grasped after I had completed it.
> It was, I found, a portion of my own self-analysis, my reaction to
> my father's death—that is to say, to the most important event, the
> most poignant loss, of a man's life.

Clearly, for Freud, the trace of Father Jakob figures into all of the other figures with which Freud surrounded himself until his own death and which now stand as a powerful (and very appropriately classical) set of tomb ornaments for the wraith of Freud in his London study. Freud significantly employed these figures to figure forth his own growing autonomy and personality,[7] and this comes across very strongly in the study itself and even in photographs of it.

Numerous avatars of the dead father serve, in a more than metaphorical way, to establish and clarify this influential theme. Following are some spectacular examples of the father figures which guided Freud's (auto)aesthetic self-development.[8]

Jakob and Sigmund had shared the famous Philippson Bible of 1858 in which, once again, "the whole past stirred," and by which we can begin to see the iconic figuration through which Freud established a dialectic of authority, culminating not only in his ongoing theoretical and analytic work, but in his lifelong fascination with the collecting of his solid figures, for himself. The young Freud had been, and of course remained throughout his life, fascinated by the figure and the figuration of Moses in the Philippson Bible, and it is to this Moses figure in Philippson, within the context of the figure of Freud *père,* that one must turn next. As he develops it

Illustration 3. The Moses of the steel engraving found in Philippson's Bible.

Illustration 4.   The Moses of Michelangelo.

in *Moses and Monotheism* (one of Freud's two "last wills," along with *An Outline of Psychoanalysis*), Mosaic religion is the *"Vater-Religion,"* the "father-religion," by which he does not at all (only) mean the religion of Jakob Freud. Sigmund's re-channelling of energy into the Mosaic mythos avoids the pain of association with the historical father and initiates a chain of surrogate, iconic father figures clustered around the figural *idea* of Moses. In his unending fascination with *the figure* of Moses Freud first explores the symbolic history into which his collection fits; in depictions of Moses, Freud perceives the liberating power by which repressions can be expressed—the artwork is the emblem and focus of that release. In the dichotomies of Philippson's depictions of Moses and Egyptian antiquity Freud felt the artist's need to impose order on a chaotic psyche, allowing art to overcome internal conflict and dangerous irrationality (Golomb 31). *Moses and Monotheism* is indeed a monument to this need, in its attempt to reconcile the *figure* of Moses with religion and history. For Freud, religion, closely related in this respect to art, is the great wish-fulfillment sublimation. Religion, however, displaces the authority of the father into a transcendent realm of infallibility after he has *failed* his sons through worldliness and manifest existence. This metaphoric figure of failed, benign, or ambivalent authority lurks in Freud's collected figures, a symbolic reminder of a potentially safe relationship with the cultural past.

The Philippson figure of Moses, however, must be supplanted by that *other* Moses, which obsessed Freud for most of his adult life, and which catalyzed Freud's thoughts on the figure of Moses in *Moses and Monotheism*. "No piece of statuary has ever made a stronger impression on me than this," Freud writes in "The *Moses* of Michelangelo" (13). In Michelangelo's riveting figure of authority Freud focused his discovery of an aesthetic beyond the genealogical, beyond the symbolic—truly an autoaesthetic. All of Freud's figurines are reminders or displaced remnants of the Michelangelo *Moses,* which represents the paradoxes through which we can begin to see, and to speculate on, Freud's relation to art: respectful yet original, attached to a tradition yet detached in a much-desired autonomy, urged to a world of order yet convinced of its impossibility at least in the realm of the unconscious. Historically, Freud's relation to the Michelangelo *Moses* is famously difficult and avoidant: he literally avoided visiting Rome and the statue for many years, in an extreme emotional response to the very *idea* of the statue, thereby establishing it as that "graven image," and thus breaking the Mosaic commandment—and, no less, for a statue erected for a papal tomb in a Catholic church. To view the statue was to commit and be caught (by himself) in another forbidden act. When he *did* see the statue, it surpassed his expectations for it and further enhanced the idea of Moses and the statue as idea. Seeing the statue amounted, in other words, to "collecting" it, adding it to those images by which to write the past and the future within the context of the self.

And yet it is in his relation to Michelangelo's *Moses* that Freud's strategic use of aesthetic sublimations begins in earnest, that the "refreshment" provided by his growing collection of antiquities first comes into play. The "value," as a father figure, of the Michelangelo *Moses* is not historical but purely aesthetic. Indeed, the aesthetic self-fabrication defined by Freud's psychoanalytic method is rooted in his response to and treatment of this piece. Freud can legitimately be seen as the son of a statue—and a function of its interpretation.[9] In "The *Moses* of Michelangelo" (1914), in preparation for which he spent many hours sitting before the statue, Freud explains to the reader that to appreciate the statue one must be able to interpret it—it must become a "readable text." And the text Freud reads in(to) the statue is an extraordinarily revealing one in terms of Freud and his figures of the father. The Moses before him in Rome becomes a very un-Biblical one, shown by the sublimations and diversions of Freud's interpretation to be not the wrathful overseer of the sinful children of Israel but the measured, rational, controlled "guardian of the tomb" (of Pope Julius II), the guardian who has "kept his passion in check" (33), "remembered his mission" (33) of protecting the Law tablets (that is, believing in metaphysical "truth"), and quieted himself to a smoldering disdain for the erring flock. Even more importantly, Freud immediately realizes his original if heretical interpretative stance as such, pointing out that his depiction of the statue is "not the Moses of the Bible," but "a quite new Moses of the artist's conception" (34). Michelangelo's *Moses*—the statue, not the "man"—is an allegorical representation not of history but of what Freud calls the fictional "accentuation" of "the power of the will" (23). For Freud this power is the *via contemplativa* rather than the *via activa,* a distinction he makes very clear in the paper. Freud thus posits for Michelangelo a role like his own: taking the material (textual and physical) of the past and remaking it through a willful and imaginative process into what it was not but now ought to be. Freud, according to his own interpretation, is the son of a representation of the power of the will.

It is within the context of the Michelangelo *Moses* that we must remember Freud's comments in *Civilization and Its Discontents* that "art" is "the employment of the displacement of libido which our mental apparatus permits of and through which its function gains so much in flexibility" (26), and that art (its creation or interpretation) is "sublimation of the instincts—satisfying because art gives body to phantasies" (26). Freud's speculation on the Michelangelo *Moses* displays how aesthetic sublimation provides a sense of autonomy, the very ground for autoaesthetics, since in the diverting of instincts the self is permitted a channel. Confronting the statue of Moses in Rome, and interpreting it, can thus be seen to be vitally linked to the "pretty dream" of Jakob Freud's death, warning Sigmund against transgression against authority; now before Michelangelo's *Moses,* however, Freud is equipped to pass beyond those earlier inhibitions, in a "satisfaction through phantasy" (*Civilization and Its Discontents* 28). Now, in light of the Michelangelo *Moses,* those eyes requested closed in the wake of Jakob's death are re-opened at another level, that of aesthetic interpretation and articulation. Freud takes on the power of determining what forces to "see" in art works. We must remember that for Freud art is itself a transference of forces (that cannot be manifested directly) to the medium in which it is manifest.[10] And as he shows in his Michelangelo interpretation, this is true not just for the artist, but "for those who are not themselves creative." This autoaesthetic power, according to Freud, is as we saw earlier the result of a strategic forgetting, a "mild narcosis induced in us by art" (*Civilization* 28) that permits Freud's much-desired "quiescence" (that is, the relief of suffering)

Illustration 5.   A statuesque Nietzsche at seventeen (c. 1861).

through a kind of Aristotelian sublimation. Thus we could speculate on the connection between Freud's treatment of the quiescent Moses and his reaction to the crisis of Jakob's death, at which time, according to a letter to Fliess, the archaeological metaphor and the theme of forgetting reached a peak. "I am working on the assumption," Freud had written to Fliess in 1897,

> that our psychical mechanism has come about by a process of stratification: the material present in the shape of memory-traces is from time to time subjected to a rearrangement in accordance with fresh circumstances—is, as it were, transcribed. Thus . . . memory is present not once but several times over, . . . registered in various species of 'signs.'

Memory is itself an imperfect system of signs, what he called "an inadequate translation" of the past. Repression is not concealment, in this model, but "a failure of translation." Although Freud later tried to replace this highly linguistic model of the memory-trace with a more psycho-dynamic one, that effort in itself is a strategic forgetting, a sublimation, and an autoaesthetic strategy.

Freud saw his "psycho-logical science" as a remedy to the chaos behind (or concealed in) art, a balance for it in the psychic world. If art unbalances, psychology (and thus aesthetic interpretation) re-balances. But this dialectic of balance and unbalance leads us to the most powerful of Freud's autoaesthetic sublimations, and the one that has under-written the preceding father figures: that of the figure of Friedrich Nietzsche. Nietzsche in fact had an enormous impact on Freud, though as would have been predictable from what we have seen, that very import caused Freud to repress the relationship and to deny the Nietzschean genealogy at various levels.[11] For Freud, interestingly, these veils of suppression or sublimation have to do with what in Nietzsche is called forgetting.[12] While for Freud art is the necessary transference of drives that cannot be manifested directly, for Nietzsche art is the remedy for science, for the "historical consciousness" whose forgetting is a prerequisite for the creative life. Thus, as in Nietzsche's collecting of small slips of paper and a few books and Freud's collecting of history, their enabling strategies were (auto)aesthetically the same.

For Freud, this autoaesthetic sublimation requires the initiatory sublimation of philosophy itself. Derrida ascribes Freud's denial of philosophy—and particularly Nietzsche's philosophy—to the fact that "what is closest must be avoided, by virtue of its proximity," and indeed the vehemence with which Freud "forgot" Nietzsche and philosophy is remarkable. By Jones's account, "Freud found the abstractness of philosophy so unsympathetic that he gave up studying it." Period. Jones then immediately declares, protesting too much, "Nietzsche had in no way influenced his ideas. He had tried to read him, but found his thought so rich that he renounced the attempt" (II 344). Jones follows this very complex (Freudian) dismissal, which so obviously contains the grounds of its own reversal, with the famous statement that Freud "several times said of Nietzsche that he had a more penetrating knowledge of himself than any other man who ever lived or was ever likely to live" (II 344). This from Freud, the founder of the science of the mind and not given to hyperbole, is not only high praise but, indeed, a confessional revelation of a father figure. Freud, like many college-aged men of the 1870s and early 1880s, had read Nietzsche's works as quickly as they were published, from the appearance of *The Birth of Tragedy* in 1872, had begun quoting Nietzsche in 1875, as Freud's letters to Silberstein show. The "richness" of Nietzsche's ideas, including *"das Es"* (the id) from *Thus Spoke Zarathustra* and sublimation, used in the "Freudian sense" by Nietzsche as early, as 1879, were by no means, as Jones wishes to claim, "unsympathetic"—quite the contrary. The minutes of the Viennese Psychoanalytic Society of April 1908, reporting on a discussion of the third essay in Nietzsche's *On the Genealogy of Morals*, hints at the fraught relationship between Freud, philosophy, and Nietzsche:

> Professor Freud stresses above all his peculiar relation to philosophy, the abstractions of which were so uncongenial that he finally decided to give up the study of philosophy. Of Nietzsche, too, he is ignorant; an occasional attempt to read him foundered upon an excess of interest. (Weber 41)

Again, as in Jones' comment on the relation between Freud and Nietzsche, we discover the telltale reversal by which we can recognize powerful influence. That "excess of interest" that caused Freud to abandon the study of Nietzsche manifests itself not only in the slips by which Freud inadvertently acknowledges this Nietzschean genealogy. In his *Selbstdarstellung* (*"Autobiographical Study"*), an exercise in autoaesthetics, Freud permits the connection to become overt: "Nietzsche," he says,

> the other philosopher whose guesses and intuitions often agree in the most astonishing way with the painfully laborious findings of psychoanalysis, was for a long time avoided by me on that very account; I was less concerned with the question of priority than with keeping my mind unembarrassed. (SE.XX.60)

"Keeping my mind unembarrassed"—these are the words of the very conservative Standard Edition—required, then, for Freud, the denial of Nietzsche's paternity.[13] Lest there be a doubt that in denying Nietzsche's influence Freud is denying "what is closest," a passage from Nietzsche's *"Daybreak"* (1881) will dispel it:

> ... need I elaborate that our drives, when we are awake, also do nothing else than interpret nerve stimulations and posit 'causes' according to their requirements? That between waking and dreaming there is no *essential* difference? ... That even our moral judgements and valuations are only pictures and phantasies about a physiological process which is unknown to us? That all our so-called consciousness is a more or less fantastic commentary on an unknown, perhaps unknowable, but felt text? (119)

Nietzsche's "guesses" and "intuitions" are indeed such remarkable adumbrations of Freud's "laborious" findings that we must see Freud's denial as his most telling sublimation—verily, in terms of Nietzsche, "you are requested to close the eyes." Freud's very theory of forgetting, as in his remarkable work on "slips of the tongue," in fact, has its groundwork in Nietzsche who, though he predictably does not build a theory of forgetting, warns that we have no true knowledge of the process of forgetting because forgetting is an alert, active, and strategic force. As Derrida points out at length in his speculations on "'Freud'" in *The Post Card,* Freud seems "simply" to avoid his debt to Nietzsche.

For both Nietzsche and Freud, aesthetics is not a matter of beauty but a *system of exchange* between pain and pleasure: art transmutes pain into pleasure, for Freud through sublimation (and on the consequent cancellation of debt), for Nietzsche through the positive embracing of suffering (Freud suggests this economic model for a pleasure/pain aesthetics in *Beyond the Pleasure Principle*). But to embrace suffering in the way Nietzsche suggests is not only impossible for Freud, but is indeed the very source and impetus of his psychoanalytic discourse. While art is a relief from suffering for Freud, for Nietzsche art is the remedy for science, for the "historical consciousness" forgotten by the creative mind. While sublimation (into antiquities, for example) is Freud's enabling strategy, for Nietzsche that role is played by active forgetting. Indeed, for Nietzsche historical study itself assumes an aesthetic guise, since the so-called Apollinian power, the rational power of the ordered dream, is a self-creative illusion. This is the root of Freud's denial of Nietzsche, and his fear of what appeared to be Nietzschean disorder. For Freud, the paradigms of mind and thought are order, science, methodology, and work; for Nietzsche, they are creative disorder, free-association, aesthetics, and style. For Nietzsche, one's "responsibility" as a human being is the attempt at a transcendence in poetic flight and image of everyday life's mundanity, a self-overcoming possible *only in metaphor;* for Freud, responsibility resides in the discovery of irrationality manifested through the drives—but then in their rational control, as we saw in his treatment of Moses. Despite the closeness of their thought—and this *is* a matter of autoaesthetic priority—we must reverse Freud's sublimate forgetting and include Nietzsche centrally among those father-figures transmuted into the figures he collected and with which he surrounded himself.

The progression from Jakob Freud to the Moses of Christian tradition to the aestheticized (and thus fictionalized and narratized), *Moses* of Michelangelo to the repressed theoretical father,

Illustration 6.   The Übermensch as machine: Nietzsche's typewriter.

Nietzsche, is a linear progression of reinterments, all requiring an excavation the first few trowelfuls of which have occurred here. But the ultimate father figure written behind Freud's collection of antiquities, embodied in numerous figures before him at his writing desk and who must not be allowed to be here forgotten, is the chimerical figure of authority, the clear, empowered, transcendent, free being beyond incorporation—the "unmasked" person (to use Nietzsche's word, or the "je," to use Lacan's) who is hypothetically also the object of psychoanalytic therapy. Both Nietzsche and Freud call that hypothetical person the *Übermensch,* or Overman: "I bring you the *Übermensch,*" Nietzsche says, "the greatest gift man has been given," the result of unmasking and thus the marriage of the Dionysian and Apollinian drives.[14] The gift of the Overman is that of the image of the hypothetically perfectible human being, at once encrypted and declared, and thus is closely linked to the various avatars of that hypothetical being, lining the walls and crowding the desk in Freud's study.[15] While for Nietzsche the overman is the always-fictional goal of the alchemical union of philosopher/psychologist and poet and for Freud the Overman is the Orderer and authoritator, from Freud's archaeological viewpoint sitting at his desk with his cluster of displaced advisors/Muses/fathers before him, Freud echoes Nietzsche's notion of the gift, writing that "The primal father was the *Übermensch.* Nietzsche placed in the future what belonged to the past" (SE.SVIII.123). For Freud, every father (indeed, the idea of the father) leaps out of the past to become the super-ego, the phantom of solidity. History, collective and individual, ideally returns us to and shows us keys to the unlocking of the hypothetical autonomous self, helping us remove our defensive masks in order to expose the illusory substructures on which we rely. Again as though anticipating (in 1873) Freud's fascination with history, Nietzsche writes out of his own fascination with it, in *On the Use and Abuse of History,* that

> only, perhaps, if history suffers transformation into a pure work of art can it preserve instincts or arouse them. Such history would be quite against the analytical and inartistic tendencies of our time, and even be considered false. (42)

For Nietzsche, only through the aesthetic power of the artist is history made *useful*. Art, in the form here of figures from the cultural past, attempts to provide the "metaphysical comfort" out of which, through the unmasking of "screen memories," the *Übermensch* approaches.[16] Through the process of active forgetting by which history is transformed into "a pure work of art," relying on its veracity and accessibility, Freud empowers history and art differently from Nietzsche to produce the Overman. Art for Freud, rather than being a system of creative and enabling fictions, represents what he called the "paleological state of man," before the interpretive act. Nietzsche would call this idea itself an Apollinian fiction, an impossible wish; *Nietzsche's* idea of art (which in fact lies masked—forgotten—in Freud's aesthetic theory) is simpler: "we possess art lest we perish of the truth' (*The Will to Power* 822).

But Freud's and Nietzsche's versions of this hypothetical goal powerfully overlap. The success of psychoanalysis and the power of the *Übermensch* respond to the same question: how much truth can one bear without retreating into defenses and illusions? Nietzschean philosophy and Freudian psychoanalysis, despite significant differences, share a common aim: self-overcoming, self-education, and the self-formation of an authentic, creative, and autonomous self (Golomb 21). But how to achieve it, this unmasking of the autonomous self? While for Freud the answer is always archaeological, concealed "below" the archaeological metaphor in another and another we can and must excavate, it is displayed directly by Nietzsche: the autonomous self is psychological and aesthetic—self-creation is a question of narratizing the self, of autoaesthetics, of style. Nietzsche tells us that to achieve an autonomous sense of self,

> *One thing is needful.*—To 'give style' to one's character—a great and rare art! It is practiced by those who survey all the strengths and weaknesses of their nature and then fit them into an artistic plan until every one of them appears as art and reason and even weaknesses delight the eye. (*The Gay Science* 290)

This is, of course, precisely what Freud did. Freud's most fundamental drive is the drive toward autonomy. In his forgetful illusion,

Freud tells us in *Civilization and Its Discontents* that this path has two conditions: first, a voluntary isolation; second, in "becoming a member of the human community" one "goes over to the attack against nature and subjects her to the human will" (24), whose goal is the happiness of quietness. Nietzsche has already laid the foundation of this idea, stating as we have seen that psychology maps the evolution of the will-to-power, which Nietzsche understands to be "a complex of sensation and thinking, but above all an *affect of command*" (*Beyond Good and Evil* 19).

The idea of the *Übermensch* teaches us that whether we attempt to command through science and history or through the artful creation of "style," the *ipse* (self) we fabricate is always immanent, always tendentious, never comes into being except as idea. At the same time, that idea of the perfect genealogy guides and defines us. The representations of an iconic past to which Freud related in extraordinarily complex ways, embodied in the iconic figures with which he surrounded himself, are self-representations in that they reflect a satisfying sense both of the connectedness and the alienation from history Freud felt throughout his life.[17] Freud's antiquities, adumbrations of that hypothetical union of history (which Freud called "fact") with the self-identifying fictions by which they are collected and interpreted, point us toward that final father figure: the impossible autoaesthetic Self whose icons stood around Freud in his study. The authoritative power of Freud's (father) figures results from the autoaesthetic discourse within which they occur, the force by which, through aesthetic sublimation, we go on writing ourselves. The Pentateuch of fathers considered here (amid others, such as Shakespeare, Goethe, Darwin) are the various species of encoded, and thus buried, signs by which Freud speculated on self and on himself, image-texts of the past written into a self-empowered future, as emblems of autoaesthetic force. Freud transmutes "figure" from noun to verb, making "figuring" the active process by which autoaesthetic power can be created. For Freud, this empowerment is accomplished through a series of steps toward self-figuration, fledgings of the heir becoming himself sufficiently powerful to figure as the source of power. Indeed, father figures in Freud's autoaesthetics.

6

Sphinx with Bouquet

Julia Reinhard Lupton

Several sphinxes were included in the 1990 exhibition of Freud's antiquities curated by Lynn Gamwell and Richard Wells for the University Art Museum at SUNY Binghamton. One sphinx, a 7-inch Greek terracotta figure, was selected for the cover of the catalogue, while another sphinx, appearing on a fragment of a Roman wall painting, was not. The choice of one sphinx over another is itself symptomatic of a certain complex of aesthetic, cultural and psychoanalytic values. The statuette, detached through photography from any sense of its actual scale, is monumental, grave, imposing; resolutely "Oedipal" in its solemnity and presence, the statuette presents a fitting logo for the institutional relationship between psychoanalysis and classical art. The painted sphinx, on the other hand, is rather girlish and sweet. Neither inserted into a narrative nor standing alone, the fragment is "decorative" in both style and function. The painted sphinx stands on a border whose undulating pattern mirrors what she holds in her hand: namely, a spray of ivy bound with a ribbon, a schematic bouquet. The graceful garland is in turn echoed in the flow of her wings, the curl of her tail, and the sweep of a hair style which can only be called a ponytail. Not only does she stand *on* a border, but she may herself have formed *part* of a border, joined by the other end of the garland to a sister sphinx, as is common in ornamental frames *à la grecque*. The bouquet in particular advertises her decorative status, since flowers are crucial elements in Western pattern and ornament. Unbound by the monumental constraints of narrative and perspectival space, and tending towards border, garland, and

Figure 1. ⸱ Terracotta figure of a sphinx, from South Italy, Greek, late 5th–early 4th centuries.

other forms of wrapping and wreathing, flowers and foliage can themselves fashion a vase, edge or casket framing a narrative within.

The image of the "Sphinx with Bouquet" serves in this essay to demarcate a Freudian "language of flowers" that traverses a series of linked distinctions between the narrative and decorative arts, botany and aesthetics, and repression and sublimation. The specimen text for the Freudian language of flowers is *The Interpretation of Dreams,* where Freud's "Dream of the Botanical Monograph" offers a bouquet of sexual symbols which manifest the ancient affiliation of poesis, posy, and sexuality. At the same time, Freud's text presses the language of flowers beyond an economy of erotic and

Figure 2.   Fragment of a wall painting of a sphinx, Roman, 1st c. A.D.–1st c. B.C. (plaster).

rhetorical substitution towards an impossible moment of pure ornamentation. Moreover, the key discourse of this dream is finally not poetry but science, the sexual science of botany elaborated by Linnaeus in the eighteenth century. The perverse sexualization of the flower under Linnean botany was registered in and countered by the emergence of the aesthetic ideology as a theory of pure form in the same century; the productive tension between the botanical and the aesthetic conceptualizations of the flower informs and helps clarify the constitutively ambivalent relation between psychoanalysis and aesthetics. Finally, botany, a sexual science dependent on collecting, offers a powerful analogue to Freud's antiquarianism,

DECORATIVE TILES THROUGHOUT — THE AGES —

Figure 3.   Sphinxes on decorative tile. Man and Company, c. 1880. Reprinted from Hans van Lemmen, *Decorative Tiles through the Ages* (New York: Crescent Books, 1988).

since the discourse of botany implicitly privileges the synchronic taxonomies of "natural history" over the monumental narratives of "art history" as the model of the psychoanalyst's collection.

Freud's "Sphinx with Bouquet" offers us the riddle of the flower—the riddle *as* a flower, that is, a figure of speech. In poetry and art, flowers have traditionally functioned as figures of signification, metaphors of metaphor. The etiological narratives of Ovid's *Metamorphoses* insistently derive the fruits and flowers of the natural landscape from scenes of erotic frustration and substitution; in these tales, the laurel, the hyacinth, or the anemone stands at once for the lost object (Daphne, Hyacinthus, Adonis) and for the elegiac commemoration of loss in a memorial bouquet, at once a funereal "posy" and an act of linguistic *poesis*. As such, Ovid's narratives offer an etiology of the erotic metaphors which are scattered like seeds or fallen petals through the European lyric, from Thomas Campion's "There is a Garden in her face" to Baudelaire's *Fleurs du mal*.[1]

Since the work of Jacques Lacan, Freud's *Interpretation of Dreams* has been read as a late flower of the tradition of classical rhetoric, insofar as the techniques of dreamwork (especially con-

densation and displacement) both repeat the mechanisms of metaphor and metonymy and spell out their relation to erotic lack.
Freud's "Dream of the Botanical Monograph" is one of several
dreams in *Die Traumdeutung* which exemplifies and analyses what
I call the "meta-florics" of plant imagery. The dream itself is brief:
*"I had written a monograph on a certain plant. The book lay be-
fore me and I was at the moment turning over a folded coloured
plate. Bound up in each copy there was a dried specimen of the
plant, as though it had been taken from a herbarium"* (SE IV:
169). The associations which follow elaborate the metaphoric relation between plant and book—between, that is, the *botanical* and
the *monographic*. "Leafing" through a book, "plucking" [*zerp-
flücken*] a volume apart like an artichoke, and failing to provide
Martha Freud with her "favourite flower" are oneiric puns which
manifest the ancient affiliation of flora and metaphor within Oedipal narratives of erotic and linguistic substitution. In the process
of analyzing the dream, Freud cites a letter from Fliess concerning
The Interpretation of Dreams; "'I am very much occupied,'" Fliess
writes, "'with your dream-book. *I see it lying before me and I see
myself turning over its pages*" (SE IV: 172; emphasis Freud's). In
the associative commentary that at once unfolds and carries on
the work of the dream, the condensation casts *Die Traumdeutung*
itself as a botanical monograph, a hermeneutics of the flowers of
rhetoric and desire.

If flowers "mean meaning," however, they also, by virtue of this
very meta-metaphoricity, point towards the limits and exhaustion
of meaning through excessive figuration, as seen in the urge of
rhetoric towards the gratuitous ornament and self-replicating patterns of "flowery language." In linguistic terms, this paradox can be
defined as the tension between the flower as a *sign* (or, more precisely, as a signifier in signification), that is, as the vehicle of rhetorical and erotic substitution, and the flower as a pure *signifier*
divorced from any meaning it might determine. As a signifier in signification, the flower symbolizes symbolization, that is, the move-
ments of the signifying chain. The aspect of the pure signifier,
however, separates out and infinitely multiplies the decorative ten-
dency of the flower from the very chain or garland of meanings that

the symbolic flower mobilizes and instantiates. These two aspects of the signifier, moreover, do not exist apart from each other. Without the ornamental "floweriness" of the flower, there could by no symbolic language of flowers, no rosemary for remembrance. At the same time, floral patterns can never really become "pure signifier" since such designs, however non-narrative or abstracted, must remain representational if they are still to be called "floral."

This distinction is repeated in the contrast between the Sphinx of narrative art—for example, Ingres' *Oedipus,* of which Freud owned a reproduction (Gamwell 23)—and the Sphinx of decorative art, gracefully joining the garlanded border of ivy and ribbon. In narrative art, the story of Oedipus recounts the drama of conquering the Sphinx through assigning her (a) meaning. The Sphinx as riddle, as question, as enigmatic signifier apart from any signified, is thus mastered by the act of solving the riddle with and as meaning. In the "Sphinx with Bouquet," on the other hand, the Sphinx appears as the neo-classical excess, *à la grecque* rather than truly Greek, left over by the classical plot of Oedipal signification; when mirroring pairs of sphinxes appear on the buttresses, cornices, and armrests of furniture, tiles, and wallpaper, their mythological significance is clearly subordinate to such decorative functions as abutment, support, closure, and symmetrical balancing. At the same time, their legibility as "sphinxes" rather than some other creature from the grotesque bestiary of ornament residually preserves the mythological reference that design de-signifies.

This distinction and dependence between the classical sphinx of the Oedipal *mythos* and the decorative sphinx of neo-classical ornament parallels the division in psychoanalysis between repression and sublimation. The classical narrative of the Sphinx dramatizes the shift, effected through *repression,* from the pre-Oedipal to the Oedipal: in Lacan's terms, the movement from the abject, incursive Thing of the real to the imaginary object of symbolic exchange and representation.[2] In this scenario, the forbidden Thing of incestuous enjoyment (the Sphinx as Jocasta) is sacrificed for the linguistic tokens of acculturation (blindness as a symbol of insight in the tragedy of castration). The "Sphinx with Bouquet," the neo-classical remainder of this Oedipal subjection, on the other hand, emblematizes *sublimation* as the movement beyond Oedipal meaning through its aesthetic hyperformalization. In Lacan's formula, sublimation elevates the object to the dignity of the Thing (*Seminar VII:* 133); in this account, sublimation dislodges or "sublimes" the object of desire into an opaque spot, stain, or doodle impervious to the displacements and condensations of signification which have produced it.

Together, these two moments posit a material (and maternal) signifier at either end of the signifying process, as its cause, its residue, and its limit. The very act of displaying the "Sphinx with Bouquet" in an exhibition of Freud's antiquities repeats the process, since the psychoanalytic context charges this decorative fragment with an Oedipal meaning and narrative direction essentially foreign to the piece's ornamental or "flowery" mode. If the "Sphinx with Bouquet" exceeds (Oedipal) meaning, however, this moment of formal excess must always be indexed in relation to the meaning which it overgoes. The point is not to put the "Sphinx with Bouquet" onto the cover of the *Freud and Art* catalogue, but rather to see what its absence from the cover indicates about the contours and by-products of Oedipal meaning more generally. It is precisely the *success* of the current cover—the emblematic precision with which the terracotta sphinx condenses the relation between Freud and antiquity—which points to the girlish insubstantiality and fragmentary transcience of the painted sphinx as the formal excess drawn off from Oedipal symbolization.

Two passages, one from Kant and one from Freud, delineate the difference and relation between the symbolic bouquet of repression which comes to fruition in and as the signifying chain and the overblown flower of sublimation which falls out from its defile. In *The Critique of Judgement,* Kant takes the flower as his first example of "free beauty":[3]

> Flowers are free beauties of nature. Hardly any one but a botanist knows the true nature of a flower [*was eine Blume für ein Ding sein soll*], and even he, while recognizing in the flower the repro-

ductive organ of the plant, pays no attention to this natural end
when using his taste to judge of its beauty. . . . So designs *à la
grecque*, foliage for frameworks or on wall-papers, &c, have no in-
trinsic meaning; they represent nothing [*sie stellen nichts vor*]—
no Object under a definite concept—and are free beauties. (E 72;
G 146; I.16)[4]

Kant shifts here from flowers in nature to the floral patterns of the
decorative arts, including not only "foliage for frameworks or on
wall-papers," but also "designs *à la grecque*"—patterns which
might very well include Sphinxes with bouquets. Kant's effortless
transition here from nature to art is enabled by his initial separation of the aesthetic object from the object (or *Ding*) of botany. The
"true nature of a flower"—*was eine Blume für ein Ding sein soll*,
what a flower is as a thing—is its function as the sexual organs of
the plant. Kant refers here to the central premise of modern botany,
the so-called "sexual system" designed during the century of Kant
by the Swedish botanist Linnaeus. For Kant, the flower can function as a "free beauty," as pure signifier and pattern, only through
the bracketing of its relation to sexuality—to sexuality as its meaning and as meaning more generally. In the name of the rose, then,
modern aesthetics in this instance rewrites its governing distinction between science and art in terms of the difference between sexuality and the beautiful.

   The Interpretation of Dreams, on the other hand, embraces
the sexual function of the flower. A dream about flower-arranging,
analysed by Alfred Robitsek and cited at length by Freud in the 1914
edition of *Die Traumdeutung,* contains the following formulation:

'sexual flower symbolism, which, indeed, occurs very commonly
in other connections, symbolizes the human organs of sex by
blossoms, which are the sexual organs of plants. It may perhaps
be true that gifts of flowers between lovers have this unconscious
meaning.' [*SE* V: 376; *SA* II 369][5]

If for Kant, the flower functions as pure form, but only at the expense of its relation to sexuality, for Freud, the flower functions as

a sign or symbol precisely through its relation to sexuality as "unconscious meaning." The Kantian aesthetics of the flower, a theory, I would argue, of *sublimation,* founds itself on the *disjunction* between the sexuality of plants (the defining insight of Linnean botany) and their beauty (the defining insight of Kantian aesthetics). The psychoanalytic hermeneutics of the flower, on the other hand—a theory above all of *repression*—founds itself on the dialectical continuity of the two realms. What is at stake, we could say, is the relationship between the Sphinx, the psychoanalytic emblem of repressed sexuality, and the Bouquet, the philosophical emblem of aesthetic sublimation.

We could thus reread the phrase "Sphinx with Bouquet" as "Freud with Kant." Following Lacan's nomenclature in "Kant *avec* Sade," I say "Freud *with* Kant" in order to counter the impulse to reduce one to the other, to correct the deluded Kantian flower with its more authentic sexual meaning. Indeed, the *difference* that Kant's passage marks between the spheres of sexuality and aesthetics may be finally, if paradoxically, more "psychoanalytic" than its classically Freudian counterpart, since it defines the structure of the signifier as a fundamental break with meaning, a break which marks a persistent non-relation to meaning while preventing any translation or reduction of form into meaning. Thus the "with" in "Freud *with* Kant" indicates at once the complementarity and the sustained disjunction between sphinx and bouquet, between repression and sublimation, between the infantile sexual research of psychoanalysis as a kind of anthropo-botany on the one hand, and the formal productions of the decorative arts as framed by philosophy on the other. Repression is "with" sublimation in the way that a woman is "with" child: that is, swollen from the inside by something which is at once radically other to yet fully continuous with it.

The "Sphinx with Bouquet," moreover, stages the difference between sexuality and art as *the difference between kinds of sexual difference:* the relation of an extra-Oedipal economy set forth by the "maternal Thing," the jug, vase or casket of the uncanny maternal body, to the "flowers of desire" of the genital organization, the objects of eroto-poetic substitution. In Freud's little painting, the maternal Sphinx, we could say, holds out the castrative emblems of

Oedipal substitution which will effectively cancel the dangerous *jouissance* that she embodies. As such, the painting graphs the structure of fetishism, in which an aesthetic object stands in for and blocks up the threatening question or riddle of the maternal Thing. Fetishism forms a pivot between repression and sublimation, since like repression, it enforces a mode of substitution, but like sublimation, it substitutes not with meaning but with form, with residual objects, cut flowers in broken vases, which repudiate the exchanges imposed by castration. Fetishism, we might say, designates the "with" of the phrases, "Sphinx *with* Bouquet" and "Freud *with* Kant." The "with" of fetishism designates a point of intimate ligature which is also a point of disjunction and asymmetry, the sign of incommensurability between the two terms it links. Thus the blind Oedipus, fulfilling his own riddle in the aftermath of his most classical tragedy, must walk "with" a cane, refigured in the prosthetic function of his deathly daughter Antigone.[6]

The phenomenon of *collecting* locates fetishism at the uncanny maternal crossroads of Oedipal hermeneutics and sublime aesthetics. The topic of collecting, moreover, "collects" the discourses of botany, antiquarianism, and psychoanalysis together in a kind of curio cabinet of arcane sciences. On the one hand, such an aggregation of modes suggests the move of historicism by pointing towards a genealogy or archaelogy of psychoanalysis in earlier traditions of science and philosophy. At the same time, the curio cabinet also represents a radically dehistoricizing gesture which isolates the act of pure assemblage entailed by collections and their taxonomies. The cabinet abstracts the act of abstraction—in the sense of removal from its historical ground—implicit in collecting; this gesture manifests the impulse not of history but of theory. My goal would be not to adjudicate between history and theory, the two drives of current academic criticism, but rather to use the phenomenon of collecting to frame their uncommon ground in natural history, the discipline inherited and transformed by the eighteenth-century botanists among others. Natural history from Pliny to Bacon included a kind of proto-anthropology, social history, ecology, and the history of technology and the arts, along with "science" in its more familiar forms. As a field which combined nature and culture in bizarre yet rigorous synchronic organizations, natural history may offer not only a promising object but also a fruitful model for the humanities today. It presents a paradigm of critico-historical investigation as materialist non-synthetic assemblage which might supplement the twin poverties of historicism and philosophy.[7] Such a criticism would arrange into one garland—a serial bouquet—the products of botany, psychoanalysis, and rhetoric, in order neither to reduce them to a shared set of principles nor to stage their avatars in a single narrative, but rather to see what sphinx-like hybrids are produced by the very act of assembling these objects and their discourses together.

In the seventeenth and eighteenth centuries, botanical collecting assumed three basic forms: the botanical garden (a living museum of plants), the herbarium (a permanent collection of dried samples), and botanical illustrations (in which the book is the museum, and the page is the shelf or case.)[8] The botanical monograph of Freud's dream includes the latter two, since it is a book whose "folded coloured plates" hold "dried specimens" tucked between them. *Collection* and *classification* were closely linked scientific activities, as every collection implied a system of organization, and taxonomy was often the goal of collecting.[9] In Linnaeus, the linked activities of collection and classification are in turn tied to sexuality, centered on the flower as the reproductive organ of the plant. As a result, Linnaeus' taxonomy guaranteed the transformation of botany from a *science of the leaf* (the ancient genre of the herbal, a guide to the medicinal uses of plants) to a *science of the flower* (the genre of the florilegia, dedicated to the blossom as the defining feature of the plant).

For Linnaeus, sexuality offered not simply a content to be classified, but the principle of classification per se. As Gunnar Eriksson suggests,

> Just as Linnaeus was acquiring his first knowledge of modern systematic botany, the basic outline of the sexual theory was revealed to him at the same time, and from the same source. . . . we may

CHAP. 26. *Of Italian Rocket.*

¶ *The Deſcription.*

1 ITalian Rocket hath long leaues cut into many parts or diuiſions like thoſe of the Aſh tree, reſembling *Ruellius* his Bucks-horne : among which riſe vp ſtalks weake and tender, but thicke and groſſe, two foot high, garniſhed with many ſmall yellowiſh floures like the middle part of Tanſie floures, of a naughty ſauor or ſmell. The ſeed is ſmall like ſand or duſt, in taſte like Rocket ſeed, whereof in truth wee ſuſpect it to be a kinde. The root is long and wooddy.

1 *Rheſeda Plinÿ.*
Italian Rocket.

2 *Rheſeda maxima.*
Crambling Rocket.

2 Crambling Rocket hath many large leaues cut into ſundry ſections, deeply diuided to the middle rib, branched like the hornes of a ſtag or hart : among which there do riſe vp long fat and fleſhy ſtalkes two cubits high, lying flat vpon the ground by reaſon of his weake and feeble branches. The floures grow at the top, cluſtering thicke together, white of colour, with browniſh threds in them. The ſeed is like the former. ‡ *Lobel* affirmes it growes in the Low-country gardens with writhen ſtalkes, ſometimes ten or twelue cubits high, with leaues much diuided. ‡

¶ *The Place.*

Theſe Plants grow in ſandy, ſtony, grauelly, and chalky barren grounds. I haue found them in ſundry places of Kent, as at South-fleet, vpon Long-field downes, which is a chalkie and hilly ground very barren. They grow at Greenhithe vpon the hills, and in other places of Kent. ‡ The firſt growes alſo vpon the Wolds in Yorke-ſhire. The ſecond I haue not ſeene growing except in gardens, and much doubt whether it grow wilde with vs or no. ‡

¶ *The Time.*

Theſe Plants do flouriſh in Iune, Iuly, and Auguſt.

¶ *The*

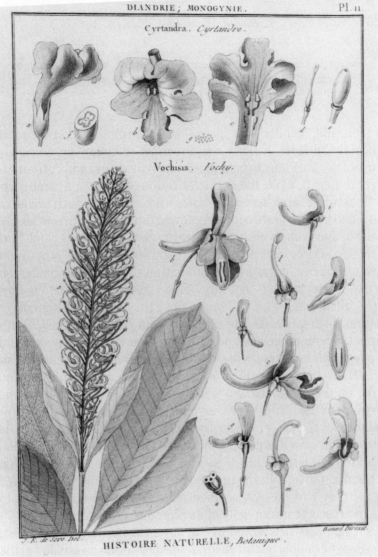

Cyrtandra. *Cyrtandre*.

Vochisia. *Vochy*.

HISTOIRE NATURELLE, *Botanique*.

Figure 5.   Cytandra and Vochisia. From Jean Baptiste Lamarque, Tableau Encyclopedique et Methodique des Trois Regnes de la Nature, Botanique. Paris: Chez Pancoucke, 1791–1823. Copy at the Cooper-Hewitt Museum, National Museum of Design.

Figure 4.   Italian rocket. From John Gerard, *The Herball or General History of Plants*. 1633. Reprinted by Dover Publications (NY: 1975), p. 277.

suppose that henceforth there would always be for him a subconscious link between the two matters—classification and the
sexuality of plants (Eriksson 65).

In Linnaeus, "gender" and "genre" are interimplicated at the most
fundamental level, making the discourse of botany an especially
provocative analogue to both psychoanalytic theory and current literary criticism. While the characterization of plants and plant-parts
as "masculine" and "feminine" dates from antiquity, such accounts
tended to be both anthropomorphic and unisexual; with one sex per
plant or blossom, a clear division between "boy plants" and "girl
plants" could be maintained. The eighteenth-century innovation
was to conceive of those functions within the same flower: stamen
as masculine, pistil as feminine. These "hermaphrodites," as they
were called, evoked moral horror, since they offered an example of
natural bisexuality. As late as 1874, John Ruskin warned, "With
these obscene processes and prurient apparitions the gentle and
happy scholar of flowers has nothing whatever to do" (cited West,
59). Many botanical illustrations from the eighteenth century
verge on the grotesque and uncanny, focussing as they do on the
"organs" of the plant. Moreover, in post-Linnean practice, the central view of the flower is supplemented by a visual inventory of its
sexual parts as well as its fruit and seeds. These part-objects function
as a kind of hieroglyphic gloss which decodes the sexual meaning
of the main image. In the process, the "organic unity" exemplified
by the flower of classical aesthetics is sublimely decomposed into
the microscopic multiplicity of its reproductive organs.

  This brave new vision of the flower as hermaphrodite must,
however, be doubly qualified. First, the new-found bisexuality of the
flower was from the beginning phallically organized around the
"masculine," "active," "impregnating" part, the stamen; a crucial
experimental proof of sexual generation in plants involved "castrat-
ing" flowers by removing their stamens (Morton 238–40). The
flower of botany was Oedipalized in the same moment that it was
sexuated; if the bisexuality of the flower perversely threatens normative heterosexuality, the hegemony of the stamen in taxonomy
guarantees the phallic regulation of sexuality. Second, the flower,

though often bisexual, is not self-contained, since in most cases fertilization occurs through the intervention not simply of another organism, or even another species, but indeed of another "kingdom": the birds and the bees that effect pollination. Thus the polymorphous perversity of the botanical flower, like that of the Freudian child, is a sign not of a carnivalesque abundance but of self-divided lack. Under the demands of pollination and the restriction of plant motility, desire and division return at the fringed center of the many-organed blossom; like Ovid's fading Narcissus, its plenty makes it poor.

If modern botany establishes a complex sexual meaning for the flower, its very techniques of collecting and classification also lend themselves to Kant's "numerical sublime," thus repeating within botany the divide which Kant marks between botany and aesthetics. The sheer number of collected objects can outweigh the effect of any single object in a collection, while systematicity can become its own principle in excess of the objects systematized. This sublime aesthetics of the botanical collection is fetishistic in character. On the one hand, it disavows the hermaphroditic flower through the emphasis on the relations between objects. It thus mimes the repressive transformation of the maternal Thing (*was eine Blume für ein Ding sein soll*) into the Oedipal object. At the same time, the sublimity of the collection taxes those relations beyond their taxonomic function by elaborating them into pure pattern. It thus enables the sublimatory elevation of the libidinal object to the place of the enigmatic Thing. In Kant's phrase, designs *à la grecque* "*stellen nichts vor*": they represent "nothing," indicating not only an *absence* of content, but an active erasure or depletion of meaning. This "representation of nothing" indicates a sublime moment which, strangely internal to the opposed discourses of both botany and the beautiful, marks their negative intersection. So, too, the biformed Sphinx materializes a sublime moment which inhabits and distorts the organic organization of the beautiful, whose gracious symmetries are so often balanced on the monstrous griffins, centaurs, and medusas of the neo-classical grotesque.

In the dream of the botanical monograph, Freud notes that the cyclamen of his day-time experience has disappeared from the dream: "There was no mention of this genus in the context of the dream; *all that was left in it was the monograph and its relation to botany*" (IV: 282; emphasis mine). In the dream-work, the phrase "botanical monograph" alludes to Linnaeus' sexual system by leaving out the cyclamen, the specific flower of Martha Freud's desire; in the process, botanical relations stand in the place of sexual ones. In effect, what remains in the dream is classification as such, the Linnean taxonomy which, as Freud recalls in his analysis of the same dream, had come to his aid in a botany exam. "My prospects," Freud relates, "would not have been too bright, if I had not been helped out by my theoretical knowledge" (SE IV: 172). Botany minus the plant, the sexual system without the hermaphrodite, the monograph without the cyclamen, leaves "theoretical knowledge" as not only the "day's residue" [*Tagesreste*] but as the *residue of botany itself.* Here, "theory" emerges not as a synthetic framework of underlying principles, but as the sublime surplus of pleasure devoid of an object that systematization produces.[10]

In his analysis of the dream, Freud explicitly links this substitution of the system in the place of the plant to the erotics of the collection. "When I became a student," Freud recalls,

> I had developed a passion for collecting and owning books . . . a *favourite hobby* [*Liebhaberei*] . . . When I was seventeen I had run up a largish account at the bookseller's and had nothing to meet it with; and my father had scarcely taken it as an excuse that my inclinations might have chosen a worse outlet. (SE IV: 172–3; SA II: 185–6)

Freud collected books (and later, antiquities) instead of some more devious activity; the term for hobby, *Liebhaberei,* literally, the love in having, renders explicit the fetishistic shift from object to system, from the thing possessed to the act of possessing it. In the process, the flower of desire materializes the differential relations of taxonomy as the sublime—because sublimely missing—Thing preserved in the aesthetics of the botanical collection.

Alfred Robitsek's analysis of the flower-arranger's dream inserted later in *Die Traumdeutung* further implicates the sublimity of the collection in an act of fetishism. In the dream, the flower-arranger recounts, *"I decorate the flowers with green crinkled paper. . . . to hide untidy things, whatever was to be seen, which was not pretty to the eye; there is a gap, a little space in the flowers. The paper looks like velvet or moss"* (SE V: 376). Fetishism, of course, in its classical Freudian formulation, functions by covering up a gap, a little space: the perceived absence of the maternal phallus. That gap, explained, interpreted, or metaphorized as "castration" through the Oedipalization of the child, is itself a flower, the uncanny organs of the phallic mother. That is, the cut flowers of castration, filled in by the velvet, mosses, and papers of the floral arranger's art, serve to symbolize the disturbing maternal realia that precede and exceed them. Those uncanny blossoms include the Biblical "flowers" of menstruation, the archaic erotics of smell mythically renounced by man's erection onto two feet, and the polymorphous perversity of the botanical hermaphrodite as it awaits the kiss of the spiderwoman. The perfume jars and funerary vases of Freud's collection, like the jug of Heidegger's "Das Ding," function in part as reliquaries for these primal Things.[11] In each case, these *fleurs du mal* designate not a fixed or idealized content, a feminine essence, but rather an indication of radical loss and *jouissance:* in the phrase of Milton's "Lycidas," the flower of the real is "a pansy freaked with jet," a flower streaked not with meaning, but with meaning's loss.

If the cut flower threatens the subject with castration, the bouquet of flowers consoles. The bouquet is a kind of Medusa's head, and the Medusa a kind of bouquet. As Freud writes in his note on the "Medusa's Head," "a multiplication of penis symbols signifies castration" (SE XVIII: 273); like the Medusa, the bouquet consoles through multiplying and arranging, collecting and classifying, the very creature which is found uncanny. In this oneiric condensation of the Medusa and the bouquet, the point is not to reduce one image to the other by showing that the Valentine's posy is "really" a nest of maternal phalli. Indeed, since such a nest never is or was "really" there, it is precisely the bouquet which fetishistically figures the maternal phallus as a primal figure, as the fantasmatic installation of a Thing lost as such. Like the "Sphinx with Bouquet," the Medusa's head is another favored motif of decoration *à la grecque;* the Medusa is as much a sublime sister as a repressed grandmother of the Sphinx, her strange replicant rather than her hidden meaning. Proudly borne on the shield of Athena, the object of prehistoric horror becomes the emblem of scientific research before its infinite dissemination in the mirrored tiles of decorative art. Thus Medusa is not hermeneutically behind or against or before the bouquet carried by the girlish sphinx; she is, sublimely, *with her.*

In the figure of the Medusa, science, art, and psychoanalysis once again converge—in the act of disappearing into—the sublimity of the collection. Moreover, it is precisely in that act of convergent disappearance that they remark the resistant difference which joins sexuality and the aesthetic by dividing them. That difference should be understood neither as the fortified frame of a reactionary formalism, nor as the permeable border of a "text/context" historicism. Rather, it designates the endless shelves and cabinets of the natural history collection. A renewed natural history of art would permit the most disparate temporal, geographic and disciplinary juxtapositions, yet refuse the syntheses of cultural history by foregrounding the act of collection as such. Collecting, both antiquarian and botanical, produces a speculative pleasure, a *Liebhaberi,* at once within and beyond taxonomic totalization: the pleasures of serialization and assemblage, grafting and hybridization, distillation, fossilization, and dessication, left over by historical and theoretical syntheses. These are the pleasures and the methods awaiting crossfertilization in a natural history of the language of flowers.

Works Cited

Alpers, Svetlana. *The Art of Describing: Dutch Art in the Seventeenth Century.* Chicago: University of Chicago Press, 1983.

Barber, Lynn. *The Heyday of Natural History, 1820–1870.* Garden City, NY: Doubleday, 1980.

Derrida, Jacques. *The Truth in Painting.* Trans. Geoff Bennington and Ian McLeod. Chicago: University of Chicago Press, 1987.

Eriksson, Gunnar. *Linnaeus: The Man and his Work*. Ed. Tore Frängsmyr. Berkeley: University of California Press, 1983.

Felman, Shoshana. "Beyond Oedipus." In *Jacques Lacan and the Adventure of Insight*. Cambridge: Harvard, 1987. 99–159.

Freud, Sigmund. *Standard Edition*. 24 Vols. Trans. James Strachey. London: Hogarth Press, 1974.

———. *Studienausgabe*. 14 Vols. Frankfurt: Fischer Verlag, 1972.

Gamwell, Lynn and Richard Wells, eds. *Sigmund Freud and Art: His Personal Collection of Antiquities*. State University of New York and Freud Museum, London: 1989.

Delaporte, François. *Nature's Second Kingdom: Explorations of Vegetality in the Eighteenth Century*. Trans. Arthur Goldhammer. Cambridge, Mass.: MIT Press, 1982.

Heidegger, Martin. "The Thing." In *Poetry, Language, Thought*. Trans. Albert Hofstadter. NY: Harper Colophon, 1971. 163–186.

Hodgen, Margaret T. *Early Anthropology in the Sixteenth and Seventeenth Centuries*. Philadelphia: University of Pennsylvania, 1964.

Kant, Immanuel. *The Critique of Judgement*. Trans. with indexes James Creed Meredith. Oxford at the Clarendon Press, 1952.

———. *Kritik der Urteilskraft*. Frankfurt: Suhrkamp, 1957.

Lacan, Jacques. *Le Séminaire, Livre VII: l'éthique de la psychanalyse*. Paris: Éditions de Seuil, 1986.

Lemmen, Hans van. *Decorative Tiles throughout the Ages*. NY: Crescent Books, 1988.

Lupton, Mary Jane. *Menstruation and Psychoanalysis*. University of Illinois Press, 1993.

Lupton, Julia Reinhard and Kenneth Reinhard. *After Oedipus: Shakespeare in Psychoanalysis*. Cornell University Press, 1993.

Morton, A. J. *History of Botanical Science: An Account of the Development of Botany from Ancient Times to the Present Day*. London: Academic Press, 1981.

Rix, Martyn. *The Art of Botanical Illustration*. New York: Arch Cape Press, 1990.

126   *Excavations and their Objects*

Sacks, Peter. *The English Elegy: Studies in the Genre from Spenser to Yeats.* Baltimore: Johns Hopkins, 1985.

Speltz, Alexander. *The History of Ornament.* NY: Portland House, 1915; 1989.

West, Keith. *How to Draw Plants: The Techniques of Botanical Illustration.* NY: Watson-Guptill, 1987.

Zizek, Slavoj. *The Sublime Object of Ideology.* London: Verso, 1989.

Notes

Introduction

1. Indeed it is much more than a catalogue. Entitled *Sigmund Freud and Art: His Personal Collection of Antiquities,* it is beautifully put together with plates of the entire travelling collection and numerous color photographs of the Freud Museum, as well as essays by leading Freud scholars. It is distributed in the United States by Harry N. Abrams, New York, and available from the Freud Museum in London.

2. See Peter Gay, *Freud: A Life for Our Time* (New York: Norton, 1988), p. 172, and the citation of this passage in Kuspit (133).

3. I develop the idea of autoaesthetics in the way I mean it here in my *Autoaesthetics: Strategies of the Self After Nietzsche,* Humanities Press, 1992. Though this book centers on interpretations of Modernist literature in a Nietzschean context, that context is so pervasive in Freud that the reference is more than apt. Autoaesthetics, the book maintains, is a strategy of self-empowerment based on distance and articulation, all the more appropriate to Freud's self-mirroring in the objects of the distant past with which he surrounded himself.

Chapter 1

I would like to express my appreciation to Ellen Handler Spitz, Ph.D. who generously gave her time to comment on this essay, and who gave me insight into this material.

1. The Wolf Man, "My Recollections of Sigmund Freud," in *The Wolf-Man by the Wolf-Man,* ed. Muriel Gardiner (London: Hogarth Press, 1971), p. 139.

2. Examples of Freud's numerous statements of this analogy can be found in *The Standard Edition of the Complete Psychological Works of Sigmund Freud*, trans. James Strachey (London, Hogarth Press, 1971), vol. 7, p. 12 and vol. 23, pp. 259–60. A rare example of Freud relating the analogy to his own collection occurs in Freud's account of "A Case of Obessional Neurosis" (*Standard Edition*, vol. 10, p. 176).

3. See Peter Gay on Freud's resistance to self-disclosure in interpreting his dreams; *Freud: A Life for our Time* (New York: Norton, 1988), pp. 124–125.

4. See, for example, Winnicott's "Transitional Objects and Transitional Phenomenon," *International Journal of Psychoanalysis*, vol. 34, pp. 89–97.

5. See also Lynn Gamwell and Richard Wells, eds., *Freud and Art: His Personal Collection of Antiquities* (New York: Abrams, 1989).

6. Reported by Freud's physician Max Schur at the end of his life in *Freud: Living and Dying* (New York: International Universities Press, 1972), p. 247.

7. *Standard Edition*, vol. 9, pp. 169–175. In subsequent discussions of the psychology of art collecting, references to Freud's classic article include: Ernest Jones, "Anal-Erotic Character Traits" in *Papers on Psychoanalysis* (Baltimore: William Wood, 1938), pp. 413–437; W. C. Menninger, "Psychoanalytic Aspects of Hobbies," *American Journal of Psychiatry*, 98 (1942), pp. 122–129; Frederick Baekeland. "Psychologial Aspects of Art Collecting," *Psychiatry*, 44 (February 198?), pp. 45–59; A. Storr, "Psychology of Collecting," *Connoisseur* (June 1983), pp. 35–36+.

8. *Standard Edition*, vol. 9, p. 174.

9. Ibid.

10. "Of Art and Language," *ARTFORUM*, May 1986, p. 128.

11. See Jones, "Anal-Erotic Character Traits," p. 430.

12. Recorded by Otto Rank in the *Minutes of the Vienna Psychoanalytic Society*, eds. Herman Nunberg and Ernst Federn, trans. M. Nunberg (New York: International Universities Press, 1962), February 19, 1908, vol. I, p. 321.

13. See note 7.

14. Interview with Robert Lustig by Lynn Gamwell. September 5, 1988.

15. Freud's maid is cited by Jack Spector in *The Aesthetics of Freud* (New York: Praeger, 1972), p. 15.

16. In a letter to Max Eitingon on February 16, 1927 (Freud-Eitingon correspondence, typewritten transcription, Freud Museum, London).

17. Lynn Gamwell. "The Origins of Freud's Antiquities Collection," *Freud and Art: His Personal Collection of Antiquities* (New York: Abrams, 1989), pp. 21–32.

18. *Standard Edition*, vol. 20, p. 48.

19. *Standard Edition*, vol. 20, p. 273.

20. See Gay, *Freud: A Life for Our Time*, pp. 15–18.

21. Freud to Jones, August 1, 1912.

22. Especially to his construction of female sexuality in terms of a male norm; this Athena has no spear, she has no phallus. (See *Freud and Art*, pp. 110, 160–61, n. 46) As a chaste and childless goddess who was born full-grown from the brain of her father Zeus, Freud's favorite statuette also suggests associations with his own unmarried daughter and most direct intellectual heir, the psychoanalyst Anna Freud.

23. In 1938 after Freud had been informed that the Nazis would allow his family to leave Austria, but the fate of his antiquities collection was uncertain, he had a friend smuggle out *Athena* because it was his favorite piece and symbolized the entire collection to him. Ernest Jones, *The Life and Work of Sigmund Freud,* vol. 3 (New York: Basic Books, 1957), p. 228.

24. On Freud's identification with Hannibal see the *Standard Edition*, vol. 4, p. 196. On Moses see Emmanuel Rice, *Freud and Moses: The Long Journey Home* (Albany: State University of New York Press, 1990).

25. For a discussion of Freud's interest in, and avoidance of, Egyptology, see Joan Raphael-Leff, "If Freud was an Egyptian: Freud and Egyptology," *International Review of Psychoanalysis,* 1990, 3:17, pp. 309–336.

Chapter 2

1. For Freud and Judaism, see Robert S. Wistrich, "The Jewish Identity of Sigmund Freud," in *The Jews of Vienna in the Age of Franz Joseph*

(Oxford: Oxford University Press, 1989), pp. 537–582, also "The Jewishness of Sigmund Freud," in *Between Redemption and Perdition: Modern Anti-semitism and Jewish Identity* (London: Routledge, 1990), pp. 71–85; Lary Berkower, "The Enduring Effect of the Jewish Tradition Upon Freud," *American Journal of Psychiatry*, 125: 8 (February 1969), 1067–1073; Martin S. Bergman, " Moses and the Evolution of Freud's Jewish Identity," *Israel Annals of Psychiatry and Related Disciplines*, 14: 1 (March 1976), 3–26; David Bakan, *Sigmund Freud and the Jewish Mystical Tradition* (New York: Van Nostrand, 1958); Ernst Simon, "Sigmund Freud, the Jew," *Leo Baeck Institute Yearbook*, II (London: East and West Library, 1957), pp. 270–305; Peter Loewenberg, "Sigmund Freud as a Jew: A Study in Ambivalence and Courage," *Journal of the History of the Behavioral Sciences*, 7: 4 (October 1971), 363–369; "A Hidden Zionist Theme in Freud's 'My Son, the Myops . . . ' Dream," *Journal of the History of Ideas*, 31: 1 (January-March 1970), 129–132; Peter Gay, *A Godless Jew: Freud, Atheism, and the Making of Psychoanalysis* (New Haven: Yale University Press, 1987), Emanuel Rice, *Freud and Moses: The Long Journey Home* (Albany: State University of New York Press, 1990); Yosef H. Yerushalmi, *Freud's Moses: Judaism Terminable and Interminable* (New Haven: Yale University Press, 1991) (hereafter Yerushalmi, *Freud's Moses*); Dennis B. Klein, *Jewish Origins of the Psychoanalytic Movement* (New York: Praeger, 1981); Leonard Shengold, "Freud and Joseph" in Mark Kanzer and Jules Glenn, eds., *Freud and His Self-Analysis* (New York: Jason Aronson, 1979), pp. 67–86.

Two works which do deal with Freud's relation to antiquity, from different perspectives than mine, are the pioneering essay by Suzanne Cassirer Bernfeld, "Freud and Archeology," *American Imago*, 8: 2 (June 1951), 107–128; and Marthe Robert, *From Oedipus to Moses: Freud's Jewish Identity*, trans. Ralph Manheim (Garden City, NY: Anchor/Doubleday, 1976).

2. *Encyclopaedia Britannica*, eleventh edition (Cambridge: Cambridge University Press, 1911), vol. 19, p. 449.

3. Lynn Gamwell and Richard Wells, eds., *Sigmund Freud and Art: His Personal Collection of Antiquities* (New York: Harry N. Abrams, Publishers, 1989).

4. Peter Gay, "Introduction," Ibid., p. 18. See Gay's perceptive section "A Partiality for the Prehistoric" in *Freud, Jews and Other Germans: Masters and Victims in Modernist Culture* (New York: Oxford University Press, 1978), pp. 39–46.

5. Gamwell and Wells, eds., *Sigmund Freud and Art,* p. 158.

6. Freud to Stefan Zweig, Vienna, February 7, 1931, in Ernst L. Freud, ed., *Letters of Sigmund Freud* (New York: Basic Books, Inc. 1960), Letter 258, p. 402–03 (hereafter *Letters*).

7. *The Psychopathology of Everyday Life* (1901), in *Standard Edition of the Complete Psychological Works of Sigmund Freud,* translated under the general editorship of James Strachey in collaboration with Anna Freud, assisted by Alix Strachey and Alan Tyson, 24 vols. (1953–75), VI, 167–68 (hereafter *S.E.*).

8. Ibid., 169.

9. Ibid., 169–170.

10. Jacques Barzun misused this piece of Freud's self-analysis to attack the use of psychoanalysis in the humanities and social sciences, asking: "If an observable, intimately known living being is to be exempt from an analysis that is not genuinely clinical, what is to be said of essaying it upon the unobservable, never-encountered dead?" *Clio and the Doctors: Psycho-History. Quanto-History and History* (Chicago: University of Chicago Press, 1974), p. 52. What is to be said is that never-encountered dead subjects are not friends and cannot have injured feelings. The difference is between a clinician's insight into a patient's psychodynamics and the patient's self-insight. That difference may constitute years of hard work on both their parts. Freud's self-reproach was not because the interpretation was wrong, as Barzun suggests, rather it was because to offer interpretations in a social context is a sure way of destroying a friendship. Freud explicitly comments on his luck in cementing the friendship together. It is his indiscretion that almost caused him to lose a friend which Freud regrets, not the inaccuracy of the interpretation. Indeed, Freud's interpretation was probably correct, or his friend would not have taken such umbrage. Cf., Peter Loewenberg, "Some Pills are Hard to Swallow," *CLIO,* 5:1 (Fall 1975), 123–127.

11. "Some Reflections on Schoolboy Psychology" (1914), *S.E.*, XIII, 241; "Zur Psychologie des Gymnasiasten," *Studienausgabe,* Herausgegeben von Alexander Mitscherlich, Angela Richards, James Strachey, IV, 237 (hereafter *Stud.*).

12. *S.E.,* XIII, 244; *Stud.,* IV, 239.

13. "A Disturbance of Memory on the Acropolis" (1936), *S.E.*, XXII, 247–48; "Eine Erinnerungsstörung auf der Akropolis," *Stud.*, IV, 292–93.

14. *The Interpretation of Dreams* (1900), *S.E.*, IV, 194; *Die Traumdeutung, Stud.*, II, 205.

15. Freud to Wilhelm Fliess, December 21, 1899, *Briefe an Wilhelm Fliess, 1887–1904*, Herausgegeben von Jeffrey M. Masson (Frankfurt am Main: S. Fischer Verlag, 1986), Letter 229, p. 430 (hereafter *Briefe an Fliess*); *The Complete Letters of Sigmund Freud to Wilhelm Fliess, 1887–1904*, trans. and ed., Jeffrey M. Masson (Cambridge, Mass.: Harvard University Press, 1985), p. 390 (hereafter *Letters to Fliess*).

16. *S.E.*, IV, 194, n. 1; *Stud.*, II, 205, n. 1.

17. Johann Wolfgang von Goethe, *Italienische Reise* (Munich: Wilhelm Goldman Verlag, 1961), p. 78.

18. The theme of the Roman Catholic part of Freud's childhood socialization and adult identity is treated in Kenneth A. Grigg, "All Roads Lead to Rome: The Role of the Nursemaid in Freud's Dreams," *Journal of the American Psychoanalytic Association*, XXI (1973), 108–26; Paul C. Vitz, *Sigmund Freud's Christian Unconscious* (New York: Guilford, 1988); and most elegantly by Carl E. Schorske in "Politics and Patricide in Freud's *Interpretation of Dreams*" in *Fin-de-Siecle Vienna: Politics and Culture* (New York: Knopf, 1980), especially pp. 189–193, on Freud's "Rome neurosis" (hereafter, Schorske, *Fin-de-Siecle Vienna*). The third act of Giacomo Puccini's *Tosca* takes place in the Castel Sant' Angelo, where Scarpia, Rome's dreaded police chief holds Tosca and her lover Cavaradossi. In the final scene Tosca leaps from the parapet of the castle terrace to the Tiber some 200 meters away. Contemporary Roman wags commented on the record-breaking long jump! *Tosca* premiered in January 1900, so could not have been a day residue for Freud's dream.

19. *Interpretation of Dreams, S.E.*, V, 422; *Stud.*, II, 410.

20. Freud to Fliess, September 19, 1901, *Briefe an Fliess*, Letter 271, pp. 493–96; *Letters to Fliess*, p. 449.

21. Bruno Walter, *Theme and Variations: An Autobiography* (New York: Knopf, 1946), pp. 164–166. See also Emanuel E. Garcia, "Somatic Interpretation in a Transference Cure: Freud's Treatment of Bruno Walter," *International Review of Psychoanalysis*, 17 (1990) 3, 83–88; and

George H. Pollock, "On Freud's Psychotherapy of Bruno Walter," *Annual of Psychoanalysis*, 3 (1975), 287–295.

22. Freud to Dr. Chaim Koffler, Keren Hajessod, Vienna, February 26, 1930, *Schwadron Collection*, Jewish National and University Library, Jerusalem.

23. Yerushalmi translates this letter, but not the Koffler cover letter nor the Schwadron postscript, in *Freud's Moses* (1991), p. 13. He cites *Freudiana: From the Collections of the Jewish National and University Library* (1973), no. 19.

24. Dr. Chaim Koffler, Vienna, to Dr. Abraham Schwadron, Jerusalem, April 2, 1930, *Schwadron Collection*, Jewish National and University Library, Jerusalem.

25. Freud, "Fragment of an Analysis of a Case of Hysteria" (1905), *S.E.*, VII, 50; "Bruchstück einer Hysterie-Analyse" *Stud.*, VI, 124–25.

26. Freud, "Three Essays on the Theory of Sexuality" (1905), *S.E.*, VII, 139; "Drei Abhandlungen zur Sexualtheorie," *Stud.*, V, 51.

27. Ibid., *S.E.*, VII, 139, n. 2; *Stud.*, V, 51, n. 1.

28. Freud to Anonymous, April 9, 1935 [original in English], *Letters*, No. 277, p. 423.

29. Schorske, "The Ringstrasse, its Critics, and the Birth of Urban Modernism," *Fin-de-Siecle Vienna*, pp. 24–115. For the building of the Parliament particularly, see pp. 40–46.

30. *Encyclopaedia Britannica*, Eleventh Edition, vol. 25, pp. 942–951.

31. Freud, "Studies on Hysteria" (1895), *S.E.*, II, 305.

32. Freud, "The Future of an Illusion" (1927), *S.E.*, XXI, 50; "Die Zukunft einer Illusion," *Stud.*, IX, 183.

33. Max Schur, *Freud: Living and Dying* (New York: International Universities Press, 1972), p. 348 (hereafter Schur).

34. Felix Deutsch, "Reflections on Freud's One Hundredth Birthday," *Psychosomatic Medicine*, 18: 4 (July-August 1956), p. 280 (hereafter Deutsch).

35. Schur, p. 351.

36. Ernest Jones, *The Life and Work of Sigmund Freud* (New York: Basic Books, 1957), vol. 3, p. 90–91.

37. Ibid., p. 93.

38. Deutsch, p. 282.

39. Ibid.

40. Schur, p. 408.

41. Ibid., p. 529.

42. Freud to Fliess, February 6, 1899, *Briefe an Fliess,* Letter 191, p. 376; *Letters to Fliess,* pp. 343–344.

Chapter 3

1. Lacan was a friend of the Peircean linguist Roman Jakobson, and on several occasions, resorted to the use of Peirce's triadic sign to explicate how, in language "there is no relation." (See Seminar of January 11, 1977, in Ornicar?: "L'insu que sait de l'une bévue s'aile a mourre.")

2. Lacan discusses this in *Seminar VII;* but already in *Seminar III,* he wrote about how the classic subject, Oedipal, constructed by reference to the signifier (around a symbolic pact, dividing ego from other, "you" from "me" on the basis of "It") was supposed to prevent the paranoia inherent in an ego-centered structure). But Lacan noticed that, even within the Oedipally constructed subject, *"A primitive otherness is included,"* so that its object is *"primitively . . . the object of rivalry and competition. It's of interest only as the object of the other's desire."*

3. I am grateful to Willy Apollon, Danielle Bergeron, and Lucie Cantin, for their important discussions at UC Irvine recently which reminded me again of how critical this passage through the other is. Recall that desire, in Lacan, is the subtraction of need (physical) from demand (the demand for unconditional love from a fully satisfying Other who will have already satisfied our physical needs):

> . . . *[T]he human ego is the other and [. . .] in the beginning the subject is closer to the form of the other than to the emergence of his own tendency. He is originally an inchoate collection of desires—there you have the true sense of the expression* fragmented body—, *and the initial synthesis of the* ego *is essentially*

an alter ego, *it is alienated. The desiring human subject is constructed around a centre which is the other in so far as he gives the subject his unity, and the first encounter with the object is with the object as object of the other's desire.* .... (Jacques Lacan, *Seminar, livre III: Les Psychoses, 1955–1956,* trans. Russell Grigg, New York: Norton, 1993, p. 39).

4. These phrases appear in works celebrating the advent of the postmodern. But Lacan's *Seminar VII,* on Ethics, sketched out the problem of equating the good with goods, precisely at the level of envy. *"The true nature of the good, its profound duplicity, has to do with the fact that it isn't purely and simply a natural good, but possible power, the power to satisfy.* .... *the whole relation of man to the realm of goods is organized relative to the power of the other, the imaginary other, to deprive him of it." (The Ethics of Psychoanalysis,* p. 234).

5. For a definition of the neo-totemic, see my recent book, *The Regime of the Brother: After the Patriarchy,* London and New York: Routledge, 1991).

6. See Jacques-Alain Miller, "Extimité," in Bracher, ed. Lacanian Theory of Discourse (New York and London: New York University Press, 1994, pp. 74–87. Pierre Naveau, Mladen Dolar, and Slavoj Zizek, *Perspectives psychanalytiques sur la politique.* Paris: Navarin 1984; and Renata Salecl, ' "Society Doesn't Exist" ', *American Journal of Semiotics* VII:1–2 (1990), 45–52. The most extensive study is by Slavoj Zizek, *They Know Not What They Do* London: Verso, 1992.

7. Speech is defined as what puts the signifier in the place of enjoyment.

8. ' *"Taboos still exist among us (. . .) they do not differ is their psychological nature from Kant's "categorical imperative", which operates in a compulsive fashion and rejects any conscious motives"* SE XIII. Freud speaks of *"(. . .) the obscure origin of our own "categorical imperative" . . . ').* [Alternative version: *'Taboo still exists in our midst . . . it is still nothing other than Kant's "Categorical Imperative", which tends to act compulsively and rejects all conscious motivation.' (Totem and Taboo,* tr. A. A. Brill, New York: Vintage, 1916, p xiv, and also p. 22: ' *. . . the dark origin of our own categorical imperative. . . . ')*]

9. *Sigmund Freud and His Art: His Personal Collection of Antiquities,* ed. Lynn Gamwell and Richard Wells, Binghamton and London: State University of New York Press and Freud Museum, London, 1989.

10. Hélène Cixous, *L'Histoire terrible mais inachevée de Norodom Sihanouk, roi du Cambodge*. Paris: Théâtre du Soleil, 1987. This appears as *The Terrible But Unfinished Story of Norodom Sihanouk, King of Cambodia*, «European Women Writers Series», Lincoln: University of Nebraska Press, *er*. Juliet Flower MacCannell, Judith Pike, and Lollie Groth, 1994.

11. Disguised as an old beggar man, the abductor has his co-conspirators imitate Rama's voice calling his brother to his aid; the brother answers, leaving Sita unprotected, except for a magical circle drawn around her. This circle is opened by her sympathy for the "beggar", who repays her charity with rape. Rama is completely powerless to rescue her; it is Hanuman and his monkeys who must confound the abductor with counter-trickery and reunite the royal pair.

12. Sigmund Freud, *The Future of an Illusion*, tr. James Strachey, New York: W. W. Norton & Company, Inc., 1961. (1927, *SE XXI*).

13. He is also husband of Maat, who speaks uprightness.

14. Why this figure should have had, together with the Chinese sage and Freud's two pet Chow dogs, a special place among the figures Freud acknowledged before reading and writing about the heart himself first inspired my speculation here.

15. "Anxiety" means here both "fearfulness about" and "anxiously awaiting" . . .

16. As Lacan put it in "Vers un signifiant nouveau", p. 8: *"There is no sexual relation, I mean in the sense where something would make a man necessarily [*forcément*] recognize a woman. I have the weakness to recognize her [*la reconnaître*], but I am perspicacious enough to know that there is no the. That tallies with my experience–I do not recognize all women. The sexual relation, there is none, but that doesn't go without saying. There is none, except incestuous. . . . or murderous."* [my trans.] *Ornicar?* 17/18, 1979, 7–23.

17. Recently Slavoj Zizek has renewed our awareness that acquiring the "symbolic mandate" is not a once-in-a-lifetime decision. It is a contract ever subject to renewal, and—to being foresworn. See his *Enjoy Your Symptom: Enjoyment as a Political Factor* (London: Verso, 1992).

18. The reality that is "advanced" civilization bars the adult (especially the male adult) from returning to infancy; the reality principle or so-

cial "Necessity" is, for the modern man, the social or moral order not untamed Nature. Hence the reversal of the telos to be found in man's primal wish today: he wishes to return to childhood helplessness, because his "helplessness" had, via his mother, been cared for. The modern daydreamer wants a return to a Mother, that is, and not to a threatening Nature, or brute reality.

The fantasy of the modern (to be situated in demand, or vis-à-vis an infinitely providential (m)Other), was not an option for early humanity, striving for "adult" independence from Mother/Nature, and escaping into desire: the Father becomes an especially important figure when natural laws are discovered to deprive us of any illusion of humanity in the workings of nature. But who, outside of Spinoza, resisted the temptation to re-establish belief in the benevolent protection of Nature, just when a new form of the father was needed?

19. In "The Relation of the Poet to Daydreaming," [1908: in *Character and Culture,* New York: Macmillan Publishing Co., 1963, pp. 34–43. (1908; *SE IX*)], Freud sees the child's play as open and completely clear about the demarcation between reality and play, and expresses "only one wish": to be grown up. The adult's daydream is furtive, secret, shameful, and expresses its wishes in a complex, tripartite structure Freud calls *ideation.*

20. See especially his "Thoughts for the Time on War and Death." It is crucial to emphasize the creative side of the everyday "art" of living in what I am saying here. Domestic bondage, infantilizing childhood, and primitivizing the "savage" are tools for enslaving women, children and so-called primitive peoples. It is precisely counter to this that I am arguing here, placing the creative side of the signifier in the hands of women, children, and the marginalized peoples of the earth.

21. In *Civilization and its Discontents,* 1927, *SE XXI.*

22. I fully agree with Thomas and Jean Sebeok's marking a distinction between apes and humans in their classic, *Speaking of Apes.* I would only point out that the researchers seeking speech in apes are unwittingly trying to find it through the ape's desire (one of the first procedures is to try to get the ape to respond to a question about what it "wants.") In the Lacanian perspective, this question—if it had a response—would index primarily the desire of the humans; it would only signify the desire of the ape if its "response" indicated its awareness that the humans could not fully satisfy its demands.

Chapter 4

1. Kuspit here seems to be following Freud's comment in "Constructions in Analysis" that the analyst works "under better conditions" than the archaeologist (SE 23: 259). Michel Foucault's early work, especially *The Archaeology of Knowledge,* tries to invent an anti-hermeneutical sense of "archaeology"; as Dreyfus and Rabinow argue, however, Foucauldian archaeology remains within a binary metaphysics, akin to that of surface and depth (94–100 and *passim*).

2. Kuspit writes, "The archaeologist is in a more impossible, or at least less secure, position than the psychoanalyst, who can, as it were, have the object of his psychological inquiry and analytically eat it too" (139). While Kuspit's figure of the analyst as consuming the object is strikingly apt, given Freud's account of the object's cannibalistic origins, it is especially applicable to Tantalus, suspended in hell's infinite desire for converting his children into food.

3. See also Derrida's *Memoires: For Paul de Man* for commentary on de Man's reading of Hegel's distinction.

4. In his 1895 "A Reply to Criticisms of My Paper on Anxiety Neurosis," Freud locates the stigmata between the somatic and the psychic, as an innate "psychical inadequacy in mastering somatic sexual tension" (SE 3: 137).

5. Lacan writes, "The double-triggered mechanism of metaphor is the very mechanism by which the symptom, in the analytic sense, is determined. Between the enigmatic signifier of the sexual trauma and the term that is substituted for it in an actual signifying chain there passes the spark that fixes in a symptom the signification inaccessible to the conscious subject in which that symptom may be resolved—a symptom being a metaphor in which flesh or function is taken as a signifying element" (*Écrits* E: 166).

6. Lacan writes, "le stigmate du réel, C'est de ne se relier à rien" (*Ornicar?* 9: 36). See *Seminar XXIII (1975–6): Le Sinthome* in *Ornicar?* 6–11, *passim.* Also see Jacques-Alain Miller, "Reflections on the Formal Envelope of the Symptom."

7. See Lupton and Reinhard, "Introduction."

8. In "The Epistemology of Metaphor," Paul de Man argues that while metaphor is supposedly based on a self-evident relationship of literal and

figurative meaning, the "asymmetry of the binary model that opposes the figural to the proper meaning of the figure" leads to an "undecidability," an anxious destabilization of the border between literal and figurative (26).

9. The passage's destabilization of the hierarchy of the archaeological metaphor not only prevents any decision between "destruction" and "preservation," but disallows their synthesis as "synthesis" or *Aufhebung*— simultaneous destruction and preservation.

10. See the editors introduction (SE 23: 256). On construction see Pommier, Fedida, and Chase.

11. Freud famously writes of Schreber's text, "It remains for the future to decide whether there is more delusion in my theory than I should like to admit, or whether there is more truth in Schreber's delusion than other people are as yet prepared to believe" (SE 12: 79).

12. For a similar genealogy, see Pommier (161–6).

13. Freud's distinction in *Moses and Monotheism* between "historical" and "material" truth does not seem operative here; I would inflect the phrase as "a *fragment* [Stück] of historical truth," emphasizing the connection of *Stück* with the *Kern* of "*Wahrheitskerns*"—"Kernel of truth" (SE 268), and the connection of both with the psychotic's "disavowed" signifiers which return as fragments of the real. For commentaries on historical and material truth, see Humphrey Morris, Cynthia Chase, and Cathy Caruth.

14. See Lupton and Reinhard, Chapter Eight, for an account of the interimplication rather than opposition of "normative" primal repression and "psychotic" foreclosure.

15. See Pommier's fine account of construction and interpretation, to which I am indebted (145–191 *passim*). Pommier elaborates a notion of interpretation as "citation" from Lacan's comment in *Seminar XVII: L'envers de la psychanalyse* that interpretation is situated "between enigma and citation" (quoted in Pommier 168). The Lacanian notion of interpretation thus includes the de-signifying work of construction; as Lacan suggests in *Seminar XI*, "the effect of interpretation is to isolate in the subject a kernel . . . of *non-sense*" (250).

16. Freud's late *Moses and Monotheism* is, of course, his own major work of critical "construction," as he himself calls it.

17. On Benjamin's notion of *Ursprung* see Samuel Weber; on "constellation" in Benjamin see Rainer Nägele. For another account of "construction" see Adorno's *Aesthetic Theory* 83–5, 316–319 and *passim*.

18. See Lacan's essay, "The Freudian Thing" in *Écrits* for an elaborate allegorical staging of the Diana and Actaeon myth. See Jacques-Alain Miller's seminar *Du Symptome au Fantasme et Retour* for November 10, 1982 for an account of the various meanings of the myth in Lacan.

19. For Lacan, the subject is more an act of *forgetting*, the falling away of a signifier, than of rememoration understood as restoration. In *Seminar VII* he states, "That which a subject originally represents is nothing other than this: he may forget. Suppress the "he"—and the subject is literally, in its origin, and as such, the elision of a signifier" (264).

20. While Susan Stuart argues for the primary metaphoricity of the collection (151), she also describes its syntagmatic seriality: "The collection is not constructed by its elements; rather, it comes to exist by means of its principle of organization" (155). Stuart argues that, while the collection ultimately is in the service of the collector's sense of self-integrity, it simultaneously "overload[s] the self with signification" (162–3). On Walter Benjamin's understanding of the collection see Abbas.

21. Thus, although Lacan argues here that the psychoanalytic object is an "imaginary point of fixation" that should be "severely distinguished" from the collector's object (135), in *Seminar VIII* Lacan reads the mysterious and "brilliant" desireousness or *"agalma"* attributed to Socrates in *The Symposium* as the *objet a* (163–78 and *passim*).

22. See Lupton and Reinhard, *After Oedipus,* chapter 7, for a more extensive reading of this passage.

23. See Lacan's *Seminar VII* on the beautiful (256; 271–81).

Chapter 5

1. See Paul-Laurent Assoun's *Freud et Nietzsche,* pp. 106–107, for a description of the development of the *Kunsttrieb* through Schiller to Hölderlin, then to Nietzsche, and thus to Freud. The relationship of artist and "nature" in this concept is vital to an understanding of Freud's view of art. The *Kunsttrieb* is a creative paradox: it is a drive derived from nature

and simultaneously a response to nature by which nature emerges through art. Elsewhere, of course, Freud explores art's relationship with hysteria (as in *Totem and Taboo*) and with neurosis. The relationship between the artist and the collector remains unexplored in Freud.

2. Indeed, Freud repeatedly refers to psychoanalysis as "recalling from the practice of art an activity that proposes itself as appeasement of non-fulfilled desires" (Assoun 257).

3. Freud's interest in philosophy was strong from early in his academic career. He joined and actively participated in a student philosophic group at the University of Vienna (circa 1874), as he told Silberstein (correspondence still unpublished). He joined this group with two friends, Josef Paneth and Siegfried Lipiner, who were both very interested in and both eventually developed friendships with Nietzsche.

4. See my *Autoaesthetics: Strategies of the Self After Nietzsche* (Humanities Press, 1992) for development of this Nietzschean aesthetic of self-fabrication. Though Freud is not analyzed at length there, the principles on which I will proceed here depend on this notion of the aesthetic fabrication of a viable notion of the self, applicable to Freud as collector.

"Autoaesthetics" entails the desired construction of an narratized self out of stories and other narratives, one's own articulation (i.e., distancing out into narratives), and the taking of power from that distance, from which one always faces the danger of anomie.

A word here also about *father* figures: insofar as collecting offered Freud a figural strategy for self-authorization and self-validation, an autoaesthetic of empowerment, I intend the single-sex designation. Athena and the other female figures before Freud in his study were, I contend, figures of self-empowerment in a male mode, within the context of (that other Freudian father) Goethe's notion of the Eternal Feminine as an agency of empowerment. Had Freud constructed a less male-oriented notion of figuration, many complaints about his treatment of women patients, and indeed the history of psychoanalysis, might be quite different.

5. Freud had throughout his life a great deal of trouble with the aesthetics—aesthetics, that is, in the traditional sense, as a definition and appreciation of the beautiful—of art objects, preferring rather, in the Nietzschean mold, to analyze them, a clear effect of the sublimation of disruptive and intimidating authority in art-objects. His response to the Michelangelo *Moses* is only the most dramatic example of this.

6. Interestingly, Freud tried over time to replace this very linguistic analysis of the memory trace, which is highly Nietzschean in design and intent, with a more energetic, psycho-dynamic one, showing that even in these fundamental and formative transcriptions of his own mental forces following the father's death, Freud had to forget his initial inscriptions and re-write them into a form he found tolerable within his new autoaesthetic strategy. Nietzsche's strategy was unacceptable: too dark, unmanageable, theoretically linguistic, and too densely philosophical for Freud.

7. I am, of course, using "figure" in several ways at the same time here. Not only does Freud's dialectic with the physical figures of Egyptian, Greek, Roman, and other antiquities involve a powerful iconic presencing of his own personality in relation to their evocative powers; they also stand as figures of empowerment through a *separation* from the past to which they in part belong. This double figuration, complicated as it is by the iden-tificatory and broader linguistic centrality of figurality itself that pervades Freud's writing, greatly enhances the power of Freud's artwork and art collecting, particularly in light of his view that art is a combination of "incomplete and dim memories of the past" (*Moses and Monotheism*, Part III, Section I) enlivened by "the image of the time" the artist has "undertaken to reproduce" and the sublimation that makes art "psychoanalytically inaccessible to us" ("Leonardo da Vinci," Chapter 6). These strands weave together not only in the artist but in the collector and appreciator of art, whose imagination and interpretive powers contribute a vital element to the aesthetic process.

8. The five father figures examined here, in some sense Freud's paternal Pentateuch, the five texts or fictions out of which to write/inscribe/assert the self *over* the father, offer provocative commentary on this Mosaic theme, since Freud's role turns out to be the opposite of the Mosaic one: while Moses exercises his power in order to exalt, Freud exercises his to exhaust and overcome the father.

9. The Michelangelo *Moses* is not only a father figure, it is a figure of identification for Freud as well: like Moses, as Freud interprets him, Freud himself becomes the lawgiver, the patriarch of a new nation of mind-scientists.

When he first saw the statue in Rome in 1901, Freud was no one and had only phantasies of acceptance; in 1912–13, when he sat by the statue for hours reflecting on it in preparation for his monograph, he was the world-recognized head of a large group of followers. Parallels between

Moses' and his role were surely impossible to avoid, though they could be sublimated into aesthetic criticism and admiration.

10. As we will see in Freud's relation not only to art but to Nietzsche, this sublimation is a function of the familiar archeological metaphor, as Freud declares in *An Autobiographical Study* (1925):

> The artist, like the neurotic, had withdrawn from an unsatisfying reality into this world of imagination; but unlike the neurotic, he knows how to find a way back from it and once more to get a firm foothold in reality. His creations, works of art, are the imaginary satisfactions of unconscious wishes, just as dreams are; and like them they were in the nature of compromises, since they too were forced to avoid any open conflict with the forces of repression. (65)

11. The objects of Freudian psychoanalysis and Nietzschean philosophy have many similar goals. Freud's desire in an analytic session was to engage the patient's narrative powers so as to break down defenses and remove veils covering hidden structures; this is the same power as that exercised by the illusory *Übermensch* which, as we shall see, plays such a vital role in the work of both Freud and Nietzsche, in such different ways, in that both test the amount of truth one can bear without erecting mental defenses (what Nietzsche calls "Apollinian fictions"). As Golomb points out, "in this respect Nietzschean philosophy and Freudian psychoanalysis share a similar aim: self-overcoming, self-education, and the self-formation of an authentic and creative personality" (21). As he often states, Nietzsche saw himself not as a philosopher but as a psychologist, and laid the groundwork for the treatment of psychology Freud hoped for and helped produce, declaring at the very conclusion of Part I of *Beyond Good and Evil*:

> Never yet did a *profounder* world of insight reveal itself to daring travellers and adventurers, and the psychologist who thus 'makes a sacrifice'—it is *not* the *sacrifizio dell'intelletto,* on the contrary!—will at least be entitled to demand in return that psychology shall be recognized again as the queen of the sciences, for whose service and preparation all other sciences exist. For psychology is now again the path to the fundamental problems. (23)

Although the way in which Freud and Nietzsche treat those fundamental problems is quite different, their mutual concern with the centrality of psychology's "path" is a deeply-shared common goal.

12. The claim of Brill and others that Freud originated the concept of sublimation is an erroneous one. Sublimation as a kind of concealment has been in philosophic use at least since Goethe. Nietzsche uses it in this way in the first aphorism of *Human, All-too-human* (1878):

> As historical philosophy explains it, there exists, strictly consid- ered, neither a selfless act nor a completely disinterested obser- vation: both are merely sublimations. In them the basic element appears to be virtually dispersed and proves to be present only to the most careful observer.

But by the time of the second volume of the same work, *Mixed Opin- ions and Maxims,* Nietzsche's use of the term "sublimated sexuality" is used in the modern sense, as are other references in later works of the 1880s, particularly in a discussion of the Platonic Eros and the *Sympo- sium* in which Nietzsche refers to the "sublimated sex impulse" (XI 259), a term also used in *Beyond Good and Evil*:

> . . . wherever powerful drives and habits prevail, legislators have to see to it that intercalary days are inserted on which such a drive is chained and learns again to hunger. Viewed from a higher van- tage point, cultures seem to require times of constraint and fast- ing during which a drive learns to stoop and submit, but also to *purify* and *sharpen* itself.

> This is also a hint for an explanation of the paradox: why it was precisely during the most Christian period of Europe and alto- gether only under the pressure of Christian value judgments that the sex drive sublimated itself into love (amour-passion). (189)

As for Nietzschean forgetting, which pervades his work, the salient passage for the present discussion occurs in *The Gay Science,* where Nietzsche addresses the nature of the creation and interpretive reaction to art. The aphorism is entitled *"The first distinction to be made regarding works of art,"* and discusses the difference between "monological art" and "art before witnesses." The difference between these two orientations is for Nietzsche most profound, since it defines the search for self in which the artist engages. The artist able to transcend the world of the witness, who "looks at his work in progress (at himself)" monologically "'has forgotten the world,' which is the essential feature of all monological art; it is based *on forgetting,* it is the music of forgetting" (367). This Nietzschean for- getting is, at another level, remembering beyond the intellect, beyond reason, and is thus linked with Freud's sublimation and his sense of aesthetic appreciation.

13. Derrida has this to say about the pain of discovery in the psychologist and its painless equivalent in the philosopher:

> What is most painful and least bearable is that that which has been paid for with so much pain (what is most painful), to wit, the laborious findings of psychoanalysis, is given to the philosopher without pain, gratuitously, graciously, as if by playing, for nothing. What is most painful is that the painful is not painful for others, thereby risking the loss of its value: counterfeit coins, in sum, produced by this unworthy ancestor of psychoanalysis. (*The Post Card* 263)

Nietzsche's painful discoveries of the connections between philosophy and psychology put him in a special category among philosophers, and clearly did so for Freud.

Freud's relationship to this suffering of discovery is itself very complex. The goal of psychoanalysis is to end suffering in the "happiness of quietness," and yet pain is a vital part of self-discovery. Freud conceals in his attitude toward suffering a very Nietzschean core, an acknowledgment of the natural place of suffering in healthy human life.

14. This is Nietzsche's word for the Dionysian and Apollinian combined and empowered, not Freud's: as early as *The Birth of Tragedy* Nietzsche refers to these fundamental human traits as *"so verschiedene Triebe* [such different drives]," always in need of, indeed whose power is unleashed in, juxtaposition. Nietzsche lays more groundwork for Freud when he declares that "our drives [*Triebe*] are reducible to the will to power" (xiv, 287), which leads him to the passage in *Beyond Good and Evil* declaring that

> all of psychology to date remained stuck in moral prejudices and apprehensions; it did not dare to go into any depths. To comprehend it [psychology] as the morphology and *theory of the evolution of the will to power,* as I comprehend it—that nobody has come close to doing yet even in thought: namely, insofar as it is permitted to recognize in what has so far been written a symptom of what has so far been kept secret. (23)

Freud wrote Fliess on 1 February 1900 that he has "just acquired Nietzsche, in whom I hope to find words for much that remains mute in me," and it is most likely that the Nietzsche acquired was *Beyond Good and*

Evil, which in addition to offering this indicated challenge to Freud and psychology is full of aphorisms about the repression and sublimation of memory as well as about the centrality of the psychologist.

15. Because the Overman cannot be rendered in a statue or an image, but pervades and "transcends" all such iconographic treatment, I have illustrated the (Nietzschean) Overman with the image of Nietzsche's textual self: his famous typewriter. As for the Freudian Overman, he/it would best be rendered by overlaying transparencies of all five images in the essay, and viewing the result. Alternatively, one need simply look at Freud's study.

16. Freud confesses in *The Interpretation of Dreams* that

> we begin to suspect that Friedrich Nietzsche was right when he said that in a dream 'there persists a primordial part of humanity which we can no longer reach by a direct path,' and we are encouraged to expect, from the analysis of dreams, a knowledge of the archaic inheritance of man, a knowledge of psychical things in him that are innate. It would seem that dreams and neuroses have preserved for us more of the psychical antiquities than we suspected. (404)

17. See Kernberg (18): "self-representations are normally integrated into a cohesive concept of the self; in short, they are 'the self.'"

Chapter 6

1. For a fine psychoanalytic account of the language of flowers in pastoral elegy, see Peter Sacks, *The English Elegy,* especially Chapter One.

2. On this distinction, see especially Lacan, *Seminar VII* and Slavoj Zizek.

3. As Derrida writes, "A paradigmatics of the flower orients the third *Critique*" (85).

4. Similar passages can be found from the same period; Jean-Jacques Rousseau, for example, wrote in his fragmentary botanical dictionary: "'If I surrendered my imagination to the sweet sensations that this word seems to evoke, I could write an article that might be very agreeable to shepherds but very bad for botanists: for a moment, let us forget about

lovely colors, sweet fragrances, and elegant shapes, and first try to obtain a good understanding of the organizing being in which they are united'" (cited Goldhammer xii).

5. Freud describes the dream's symbolism as "*hübsche*," beautiful, indicating the affinity of the dream to the aesthetic.

6. On *Oedipus at Colonus* as a post-classical tragedy, see Felman, "Beyond Oedipus," and Lupton and Reinhard.

7. See Svetlana Alpers, *The Art of Describing*, on the relevance of natural history not only to the art of the seventeenth century, but to art historiography more generally. On sixteenth-century anthropology as natural history, see Hogden. On natural history in the period preceding Freud, see Barber. Walter Benjamin's work sets into motion a modern model of criticism as natural history.

8. Morton 121–5. On botanical illustration, see Martyn Rix, *The Art of Botanical Illustration*.

9. Supported by the technologies of exploration, Linneaus is said to have studied over 7000 different species in developing his "sexual system" (Morton 260).

10. In "Instincts and their Vicissitudes," Freud distinguishes sublimation from idealization: "In so far as sublimation describes something that has to do with the instinct and idealization something to do with the object, the two concepts are to be distinguished from one another" (SE XIV: 94).

11. On the psychoanalytic language of flowers as a language of menstruation, and the archaic links between menstruation and smell, see Mary Jane Lupton's chapter on "Menstrual Representations: Flowers and Floods."

Bibliography

Abbaas, Ackbar. "Walter Benjamin's Collector: The Fate of Modern Experience." *New Literary History* 20 (Autumn 1988), 217–37.

Adorno, Theodor. *Aesthetic Theory*. Trans. C. Lenhardt. New York: Routledge & Kegan Paul, 1984.

Alpers, Svetlana. *The Art of Describing: Dutch Art in the Seventeenth Century*. Chicago: The University of Chicago Press, 1983.

Assoun, Paul-Laurent. *Freud et Nietzsche*. Paris: Presses Universitaires de France, 1980.

Austin, J.L. *How To Do Things With Words*. Second edition, ed. by J.O. Urmson et al. Cambridge: Harvard University Press, 1962.

Bakan, David. *Sigmund Freud and the Jewish Mystical Tradition*. New York: Van Nostrand, 1958.

Baekeland, Frederick. "Psychological Aspects of Art Collecting." *Psychiatry*. 44 (February 198?), 45–59.

Barber, Lynn. *The Heyday of Natural History, 1820–1870*. Garden City, New York: Doubleday, 1980.

Barker, Stephen. *Autoaesthetics: Strategies of the Self After Nietzsche*. Atlantic Heights, New Jersey: The Humanities Press, 1991.

Barzun, Jacques. *Clio and the Doctors: Psycho-History, Quanto-History, and History*. Chicago: The University of Chicago Press, 1974.

Benjamin, Walter. "Eduard Fuchs, Collector and Historian." In *One Way Street and Other Writings*. Trans. Edmund Jephcott and Kingsley Shorter. London: Verso, 1979. 349–86.

———. *Gesammelte Schriften*. Frankfurt: Suhrkamp Verlag, 1977.

──────. "Unpacking My Library." In *Illuminations*. Ed. Hannah Arendt, trans. Harry Zohn. New York: Schocken Books, 1969.

Bergman, Martin S. "Moses and the Evolution of Freud's Jewish Identity." *Israel Annals of Psychiatry and Related Disciplines* 14:1 (March 1976), 3–26.

Berkower, Larry. "The Enduring Effect of the Jewish Tradition Upon Freud." *American Journal of Psychiatry* 125:8 (February 1969), 1067–73.

Bernfeld, Suzanne Cassirer. "Freud and Archaeology." *American Imago* 8:2 (June 1951), 107–128.

Caruth, Cathy. "Traumatic Departures: Survival and History in Freud." Unpublished paper.

Chase, Cynthia. "Translating the Transference: Psychoanalysis and the Construction of History." In Smith, Ed. 103–26.

Cixous, Hélène. *L'Histoire terrible mais inachevée de Norodom Sihanouk, roi du Cambodge*. Paris: Théâtre du Soleil, 1987.

Delaporte, Françoise. *Nature's Second Kingdom: Explorations of Vegetality in the Eighteenth Century*. Trans. Arthur Goldhammer. Cambridge, Massachusetts: MIT Press, 1982.

de Man, Paul. "The Epistemology of Metaphor." In *On Metaphor*. Ed. Sheldon Sacks. Chicago: The University of Chicago Press, 1979, 11–28.

──────. "Sign and Symbol in Hegel's *Aesthetics*." *Critical Inquiry* 8:4 (Summer 1982): 761–75.

Derrida, Jacques. *Memoires: For Paul de Man*. Trans. Cecile Lindsay, et al. New York: Columbia University Press, 1986.

──────. *The Post Card: From Socrates to Freud and Beyond*. Trans. Alan Bass. Chicago: The University of Chicago Press, 1987.

──────. *The Truth in Painting*. Trans. Geoff Bennington and Ian McLeod. Chicago: The University of Chicago Press, 1987.

Deutsch, Felix. "Reflections on Freud's One Hundredth Birthday." *Psychosomatic Medicine* 18:4 (July-August 1956), 280.

Dreyfus, Hubert L. and Paul Rabinow. *Michel Foucault: Beyond Structuralism and Hermeneutics*. Chicago: The University of Chicago Press, 1982.

Ericksson, Gunnar. *Linneaus: The Man and His Work*. Ed. Tore Faängsmyr. Berkeley: University of California Press, 1983.

Fedida, Pierre. "La Construction (introduction à une question de la mémoire dans la supervision)." *Révue Française de Psychanalyse* 19:1 (July-August 1985), 1141–49.

Felman, Shoshana. "Beyond Oedipus." In *Jacques Lacan and the Adventure of Insight*. Cambridge: Harvard University Press, 1987, 99–159.

Foucault, Michel. *The Archaeology of Knowledge*. Trans A.M. Sheridan Smith. New York: Pantheon Books, 1972.

Freud, Sigmund. *An Autobiographical Study*. SE XX:7–70.

———. *Beyond the Pleasure Principle*. SE XVIII:7–64.

———. "The Relation of the Poet to Daydreaming." In *Character and Culture*. New York: Macmillan Publishing, 1963.

———. *Civilization and Its Discontents*. Ed. and trans. James Strachey. New York: W.W. Norton, 1961.

———. *The Complete Letters of Sigmund Freud to Wilhelm Fliess, 1887–1904*. Ed. and trans. Jeffrey Moussaieff Masson. Cambridge: Harvard University Press, 1985.

———. *The Future of an Illusion*. Trans. James Strachey. New York: W.W. Norton, 1961.

———. *The Interpretation of Dreams*. Trans. A. A. Brill. New York: The Modern Library (Random House), 1978.

———. *The Interpretation of Dreams*. SE IV.

———. *Letters of Sigmund Freud*. Ed. Ernst L. Freud. Trans. Tania Stern and James Stern. New York: Basic Books, 1960.

———. *Moses and Monotheism: Three Essays*. SE XXIII:7–137.

———. *The Standard Edition of the Compete Psychological Works of Sigmund Freud*. Ed. and Trans. James Strachey. 24 vols. London: The Hogarth Press, 1953–74.

———. *Studienausgabe*. 14 vols. Frankfurt: Fischer Verlag.

———. *Totem and Taboo*. Trans. A. A. Brill. New York: Vintage, 1916.

———. *Zwei Falldarstellungen*. Frankfurt: Fischer Verlag, 1982.

————. and Breuer, Josef. *Studien Über Hysterie*. Frankfurt: Fisher Verlag, 1970.

Gamwell, Lynn and Richard Wells, eds. *Sigmund Freud and Art: His Personal Collection of Antiquities*. Albany: State University of New York Press, 1989.

————. "The Origins of Freud's Antiquities Collection." *In Freud and Art: His Personal Collection of Antiquities*. 31–32.

Garcia, Emanuel E. "Somatic Interpretation in a Transference Cure: Freud's Treatment of Bruno Walter." *International Review of Psychoanalysis* 17 (1990) 3, 83–88.

Gay, Peter. *Freud: A Life for Our Time*. New York: W.W. Norton, 1988.

————. *Freud, Jews, and Other Germans: Masters and Victims in Modernist Culture*. New York: Oxford University Press, 1978.

————. *A Godless Jew: Freud, Atheism, and the Making of Psychoanalysis*. New Haven: Yale University Press, 1987.

Goethe, Johann Wolfgang von. *Italienische Reise*. Munich: Wilhelm Goldmann Verlag 1961.

Golomb, Jacob. *Nietzsche's Enticing Psychology of Power*. Ames, Iowa: Iowa State University Press, 1989.

Grigg, Kenneth A. "All Roads Lead to Rome: The Role of the Nursemaid in Freud's Dreams." *Journal of the American Psychoanalytic Association*. XXI (1973), 108–26.

Heidegger, Martin. "The Thing." In *Poetry, Language, Thought*. Trans. Albert Hofstadter. New York: Harper Colophon, 1971. 163–186.

Hodgen, Margaret T. *Early Anthropology in the Sixteenth and Seventeenth Centuries*. Philadelphia: Univ. of Pennsylvania Press, 1964.

Jones, Ernest. "Anal-Erotic Character Traits." In *Papers on Psychoanalysis*. Baltimore: William Wood, 1938. 413–37.

————. *The Life and Work of Sigmund Freud*. New York: Basic Books, 1957.

Kant, Emmanuel. *The Critique of Judgement*. Trans. with indexes by James Creed Meredith. Oxford at the Clarendon House, 1952.

————. *Kritik der Urteilskraft*. Frankfurt: Suhrkamp, 1957.

Kaplan, Abraham. "Freud and Modern Philosophy." *Freud and the 20th Century*. Ed. Benjamin Nelson. New York: Meridian Books, 1961. 209–29.

Kernberg, Otto F. "The Dynamic Unconscious." *Theories of the Unconscious and Theories of the Self*. Ed. Raphael Stern. Hillsdale, N.J.: The Analytic Press, 1987. 3–26.

Klein, Dennis B. *Jewish Origins of the Psychoanalytic Movement*. New York: Praeger, 1981.

Kofman, Sarah. *The Childhood of Art: An Interpretation of Freud's Aesthetics*. Trans. Winifred Woodhull. New York: Columbia University Press, 1988.

Krüll, Marianne. *Freud and His Father*. Trans. Arnold J. Pomerans. New York: W.W. Norton, 1986.

Kuspit, Donald, "A Mighty Metaphor: The Analogy of Archaeology and Psychoanalysis." In Gamwell, ed. 133–51.

Lacan, Jacques. *Écrits*. Paris: Éditions du Seuil, 1966.

———. *Écrits: A Selection*. *Trans. Alan Sheridan*. New York: Norton, 1977.

———. "Science and Truth." Trans. from *Écrits* by Bruce Fink. *Newsletter of the Freudian Field* 3.1&2 (1989), 4–29.

———. *Le Séminaire, Livre III: Les Psychoses, 1955–1956*. Trans. Russell Grigg. New York: Norton, 1993.

———. *Le Séminaire, Livre VII: L'éthique de la psychanalyse*. Text established by Jacques-Alain Miller. Paris: Éditions du Seuil, 1986.

———. *Le Séminaire, Livre VIII: Le transfert*. Text established by Jacques-Alain Miller. Paris: Éditions du Seuil, 1991.

———. *Le Séminaire, Livre XXIII: Le sinthome*. Text established by Jacques-Alain Miller. *Ornicar?* 6 (1976) 3–20; 7 (1976) 3–18; 8 (1976) 6–20; 9 (1977) 32–40; 10 (1977) 5–12; 11 (1977) 2–9.

Lemmen, Hans van. *Decorative Tiles Throughout the Ages*. New York: Crescent Books, 1988.

Loewenberg, Peter. "A Hidden Zionist Theme in Freud's 'My Son, the Myops . . .' Dream." *Journal of the History of Ideas*. 31:1 (January-March 1970), 129–32.

————. "Sigmund Freud as a Jew: A Study in Ambivalance and Courage." *Journal of the History of the Behavioral Sciences* 7:4 (October 1971), 129–32.

————. "Some Pills Are Hard to Swallow." *Clio* 5:1 (Fall 1975), 123–27.

Lupton, Julia Reinhard and Kenneth Reinhard. *After Oedipus: Shakespeare in Psychoanalysis*. Ithaca, New York: Cornell University Press, 1993.

Lupton, Mary Jane. *Menstruation and Psychoanalysis*. Urbana: University of Illinois Press, 1993.

MacCannell, Juliet Flower. *The Regime of the Brother: After the Patriarchy*. London and New York: Routledge, 1991.

Menninger, W.C. "Psychoanalytic Aspects of Hobbies." In *American Journal of Psychiatry*. 98 (1942), 122–29.

Miller, Jacques-Alain. *Du Symptome au Fantasme et Retour*. Unpublished seminar transcript, 1982.

————. "Reflections on the Formal Envelope of the Symptom." *lacanian ink* 4 (Fall 1991), 13–22.

Morris, Humphrey. "Translating Transmission: Representation and Enactment in Freud's Construction of History." In Smith, ed. 48–102.

Morton, A.G. *History of Botanical Science: An Account of the Development of Botany from Ancient Times to the Present Day*. London: Academic Press, 1981.

Nägele, Rainer. *Theatre, Theory, Speculation: Walter Benjamin and the Scenes of Modernity*. Baltimore: The Johns Hopkins University Press, 1991.

Naveau, Pierre, Mladen Dolar, and Slavoj Zizek. *Perspectives psychanalytiques sur la politique*. Paris: Navarin, 1984.

Nelson, Benjamin, ed. *Freud and the 20th Century*. New York: Meridian Books, 1961.

Nietzsche, Friedrich. *Beyond Good and Evil*. Trans. Walter Kaufmann. New York: Vintage Books, 1966.

————. *Daybreak*. Trans. R.J. Hollingdale. Cambridge: Cambridge University Press, 1982.

————. *The Gay Science*. Trans. Walter Kaufmann. New York: Vintage Books, 1974.

————. *On the Genealogy of Morals*. Trans. Walter Kaufmann. New York: Vintage Books, 1969.

————. *Human, All-too-human*. Trans. Marion Faber. Lincoln: University of Nebraska Press, 1984.

————. *The Use and Abuse of History*. Trans. Adrian Collins. Indianapolis: The Library of Liberal Arts (Bobbs-Merrill Educational Publishing), 1979.

————. *The Will to Power*. Trans. Walter Kaufmann and R. J. Hollingdale. New York: Vintage Books, 1968.

"Of Art and Language." Artforum. May 1986, 128.

Pollock, George H. "On Freud's Psychotherapy of Bruno Walter." *Annual of Psychoanalysis* 3 (1975), 287–95.

Pommier, Gerard. *Le Dénouement d'une analyse*. Paris: Point Hors Ligne, 1987.

Rank, Otto. *Minutes of the Vienna Psychoanalytic Society*. Trans. M. Nunberg. Eds. Herman Nunberg and Ernst Federn. New York: International University of New York, 1990.

Raphael-Leff, Joan. "If Freud was an Egyptian: Freud and Egyptology." In *International Review of Psychoanalysis*, 1990, 3:17, 309–336.

Rice, Emmanuel. *Freud and Moses: The Long Journey Home*. Albany: State University of New York Press, 1990.

Rickels, Laurence, ed. *Looking After Nietzsche*. Albany: State University of New York Press, 1991.

Rix, Martyn. *The Art of Botanical Illustration*. New York: Arch Cape Press, 1990.

Robert, Marthe. *From Oedipus to Moses: Freud's Jewish Identity*. Trans. Ralph Manheim. Garden City, N.Y.: Anchor Doubleday, 1976.

Sacks, Peter. *The English Elegy: Studies in the Genre from Spenser to Yeats*. Baltimore: The Johns Hopkins University Press, 1985.

Schorske, Carl E. "Politics and Patricide in Freud's *Interpretation of Dreams*." In *Fin-de Siècle Vienna: Politics and Culture*. New York: Knopf, 1980.

Schur, Max. *Freud: Living and Dying. New York: International Universities Press, 1972.*

Shengold, Leonard. "Freud and Joseph." In *Freud and His Self-Analysis*. Mark Kanzer and Jules Glenn, eds. New York: Jason Aronson, 1979.

Simon, Ernst. "Sigmund Freud, the Jew." *Leo Baeck Institute Yearbook II. London: East and West Library, 1957.*

Smith, Joseph H. and Humphrey Morris, eds. *Telling Facts: History and Narration in Psychoanalysis*. Baltimore: The Johns Hopkins University Press, 1992.

Spector, Jack. *The Aesthetics of Freud*. New York: Praeger, 1972.

Speltz, Alexander. *The History of Ornament*. New York: Portland House, 1915; 1989.

Spence, Donald P. *The Freudian Metaphor: Toward Paradigm Change in Psychoanalysis*. New York and London: Norton, 1987.

Storr, A. "Psychology of Collecting." In *Connoisseur*. (June 1983), 35–36+. Universities Press, 1962. February 19, 1908, V. I, 321.

Stuart, Susan. *On Longing: Narrative of the Miniature, the Gigantic, the Souvenir, the Collection*. Baltimore: The Johns Hopkins University Press, 1984.

Vitz, Paul C. *Sigmund Freud's Christian Unconscious*. New York: Guilford, 1988.

Walter, Bruno. *Theme and Variations: An Autobiography*. New York: Knopf, 1946.

Weber, Samuel. "Genealogy of Modernity: History, Myth, and Allegory in Benjamin's *Origin of the German Mourning Play*." *MLN* 106:3 (April 1991). 465–500.

———. *Return to Freud: Lacan's Dislocation of Psychoanalysis*. New York: Cambridge University Press, 1991.

West, Keith. *How to Draw Plants: The Techniques of Botanical Illustration*. New York: Watson-Guptill, 1987.

Winnicott, D.W. "Transitional Objects and Transitional Phenomenon." In *International Journal of Psychoanalysis* V. 34 (89–97).

Wistrich, Robert S. "The Jewish Identity of Sigmund Freud." In *The Jews of Vienna in the Age of Franz Joseph*. Oxford: Oxford University Press, 1989.

———. "The Jewishness of Sigmund Freud." In *Between Redemption and Perdition: Modern Antisemitism and Jewish Identity*. London: Routledge, 1990.

Wolf Man, The. "My Recollections of Sigmund Freud." In *The Wolf-man by the Wolf-man*. Ed. Muriel Gardiner. London: Hogarth Press, 1971.

Yerushalmi, Yosef H. *Freud's Moses: Judaism Terminable and Interminable*. New Haven: Yale University Press, 1991.

Zizek, Slavoj. *Enjoy Your Symptom: Enjoyment as a Political Factor*. London: Verso, 1992.

———. *The Sublime Object of Ideology*. London: Verso, 1989.

———. *They Know Not What They Do*. London: Verso, 1992.

Contributors

Stephen Barker is Associate Dean and Director of the School of the Arts Program in Interdisciplinary Studies at the University of California, Irvine. He is the author of *Autoaesthetics: Strategies of the Self After Nietzsche* (1992) and has edited *Signs of Change: Premodern* -> Modern -> Postmodern (1995) and *Bodytheory* (forthcoming) in addition to numerous essays on Nietzsche, Derrida, Beckett, Arthur Miller, Blanchot, Faulkner, Jarry, and others, and on literary, performance, and Postmodern theory. He is finishing a volume on Beckett and an anthology of performance theory.

Lynn Gamwell is an art historian, Director of the Art Museum at SUNY—Binghamton, and organizer of an exhibition series on Art and Science in cooperation with the New York Academy of Sciences in Manhattan. She curated *Sigmund Freud Antiquities: Fragments from a Buried Past,* the first exhibition of Freud's personal art collection, which toured the United States and catalyzed this volume. She is co-author, with medical historian Nancy Tomes, of *Madness in America: Cultural and Medical Perceptions of Mental Illness Before 1914* (1995).

Peter Loewenberg teaches history at UCLA, is on the faculty of the Southern California Psychoanalytic Institute, and has a private practice as a psychoanalyst. He is the author of over one hundred papers on German and Austrian history, European cultural and intellectual history, and psychohistory, and of several books, including *Decoding the Past: the Psychohistorical Approach* (1983; 1985) and *Psychology and Historical Interpretation* (1988).

Julia Reinhard Lupton teaches English and comparative literature at the University of California, Irvine. She is co-author, with Kenneth Reinhard, of *After Oedipus: Shakespeare in Psychoanalysis* (1993), and author of *Afterlives of the Saints: Hagiography, Typology, and Renaissance Literature* (forthcoming).

Juliet Flower MacCannell teaches English and comparative literature at the University of California, Irvine. She is the author of *Figuring Lacan* (1986), co-author, with Dean MacCannell, of *The Time of the Sign: A Semiotic Interpretation of Modern Culture* (1982), and editor of *The Regime of the Brother: After the Patriarchy* (1992) and *Thinking Bodies* (co-edited with Laura Zakarin; 1994). Along with Judith Pike and Lollie Groth, she translated Hélène Cixous' *The Terrible But Unfinished Story of Norodom Sihanouk, King of Cambodia* (1993). She was co-editor of *Feminism and Psychoanalysis: A Critical Dictionary* (1993). She has published essays on Stendhal, feminine *jouissance,* Hannah Arendt, Foucault, Baudrillard, ethnic cleansing, Lacan and love, and woman's speech, all from the psychoanalytic viewpoint.

Kenneth Reinhard teaches English at UCLA. He is co-author, with Julia Reinhard Lupton, of *After Oedipus: Shakespeare in Psychoanalysis.* He is currently working on a book on the Neighbor in theology, philosophy, and psychoanalysis.

Index

Adler, Alfred, 8
Alpers, Svetlana, 147 n. 7
Apollon, Willy, 134 n. 3
Assoun, Paul-Laurent, 140 n. 1
Athena, 129 n. 22
Austin, J. L., 69

Baboon of Thoth, 6
Bacon, Francis, 116
Baekeland, Frederick, 128 n. 7
Bakar, David, 130 n. 1
Barker, Stephen, xviii, 81–106
Barzun, Jacques, 131 n. 10
Baudelaire, Charles, 110
Benjamin, Walter, xvii, 73–74, 79,
    140 n. 17, 147 n. 7
Bergeron, Danielle, 134 n. 3
Bergman, Martin S., 130 n. 1
Berkower, Lary, 130 n. 1
Bernfeld, Suzanne Cassirer,
    130 n. 1
Beuys, Joseph, 4
Breuer, Joseph, 7, 61–63
Brücke, Ernst, 23

Campion, Thomas, 110
Cantin, Lucie, 134 n. 3
Charcot, Jean Martin, 62
Cixous, Hélène, 43, 136 n. 10

Darwin, Charles, 36, 43, 106
Deleuze, Gilles, 36
Derrida, Jacques, 83, 100, 102,
    138 n. 3, 146 n. 3

Descartes, René, 56
Deutsch, Felix, 30, 133 n. 34, 134 n. 38

Eitingon, Max, 129 n. 16
Eriksson, Gunnar, 117, 120

Felman, Shoshona, 147 n. 6
Fliess, Wilhelm, 23, 83, 90, 91, 97–98,
    132 n. 15, 132 n. 20, 134 n. 42
Foucault, Michel, 138 n. 1
Freud, Anna, viii, 129 n. 22
Freud, Ernst, 131 n. 6
Freud, Jakob, vii, xviii, 18–19, 87–92,
    97, 102
Freud, Martha, 122
Freud, Sigmund, and:
    addiction, 3
    his theory of collecting, 2–12
    the archaeological metaphor,
        xii–xiii, 57–79
    the Acropolis, 19
    cancer, 30–32
    the Castel Sant' Angelo, 20–23
    ego, x–xi, 55
    Egyptian god figures, 10–12
    Epictetus, 29
    father figures, xviii–xix, 52–56,
        81–106
    Greek god figures, 2–6, 17
    Greek mythology, 17–18
    Judaism, 13–32
    memory, 84–85
    Moses, 22
    Seneca, 29

161